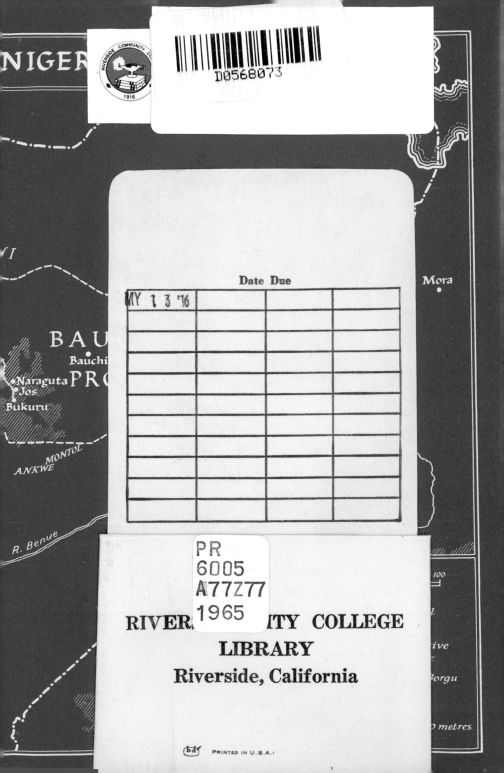

Joyce Cary's Africa

Joyce Cary's Africa

M. M. Mahood

Houghton Mifflin Company, Boston

The Riverside Press, Cambridge

1965

First Printing C
First American Edition 1965
Copyright © 1964 by M. M. Mahood
All rights reserved including the right to
reproduce this book or parts thereof in any form
Library of Congress Catalog Card Number: 64-23573
Printed in the United States of America

Foreword

At the very beginning of his career as a novelist, Joyce Cary regretted that it was not possible to learn the writer's craft in the way that an art student learns the painter's, by watching a master hand at work. Today, the student of literature can in fact watch Cary himself at work, thanks to Mr. James Osborn's permanent loan to the Bodleian Library of all the novelist's manuscripts. This collection includes Cary's many manuscript drafts and working notes for each novel, together with notebooks containing a great number of rough sketches which he used as material for his books. The series of journal-letters which Joyce Cary wrote to his wife during his Nigerian service, and which is also in the Osborn collection, is such a full and immediate record of his life in Africa that anyone reading these letters today feels he is in possession of the scene that Cary painted in *Aissa Saved* and *Mister Johnson*.

The analogy with painting is not, of course, complete. An acquaintance with the scene itself, a sight of the sketches and a study of the work in all its stages must not mislead us into thinking that Cary set about writing novels of Nigerian life in exactly the way Constable set about painting Dedham Vale. In his Clark Lectures, Cary described the process by which the sight of a girl on a Manhattan boat became a short story that had nothing to do with Manhattan nor, ostensibly, with that particular girl. I have tried in this book to keep in mind this warning against too facile an association of a writer's adventures with his work, and have therefore separated my account of Cary's life in Nigeria from my discussion of his novels with an African background. In this way I hope to have given the reader the chance to test both the reliability and the validity of such connexions between the life and the work as I have attempted, and to discover others which I have missed.

Page references to Cary's novels are taken from the collected 'Carfax' edition published by Michael Joseph. The abbreviation 'MS' after a quotation indicates that it is from the manuscript drafts of the novel concerned in the James Osborn collection. Numbers other than page numbers refer to the notebooks, which are in the process of being arranged and catalogued by Mrs Barbara Fisher. I am very grateful to Mrs Fisher for making these means of identification available to me. Articles, published or unpublished, are referred to by a brief title in the text; a fuller description can be found in the list of sources at the end of the book. This list also makes clear my indebtedness to Joyce Cary's family, friends and former colleagues, who have all given me ready and kindly help. I am particularly grateful to Mrs D. Davin, Joyce Cary's literary executor, for arranging for me to have full access to the manuscripts and for her continued interest in this study. Like all admirers of Cary, I am very appreciative of Mr James Osborn's generosity in making the Cary manuscripts available to readers at the Bodleian Library.

Ibadan, Nigeria   M. M. MAHOOD

Contents

Illustrations

The drawings in the text are all reproduced from Joyce
Cary's letters.

Fact

Gombe and the Cameroons
1914 – 1916

I

Joyce Cary joined the Nigerian Political Service towards the end of 1913, when he was twenty-five. Why he did so is not clear, and perhaps was never wholly clear to Cary himself. But a reason which must have been to the forefront of his mind at the time was the need to prove, both to his own family and to the family of Gertrude Ogilvie, whom he hoped to marry, that he could hold a steady job. To the staider members of the large, settled Ogilvie family, Cary's career since he had left school in 1905 spelt instability. Certainly it had not given him any chance to gather moss. 'You know how easily I do succumb to temptation', he wrote to his wife in 1919. 'How I left school for France, France for Edinburgh, the Art School for writing, writing for Oxford, Oxford for Store Street, Store Street for Montenegro, Montenegro for Ireland, and then Ireland for Nigeria' (31 May 1919).

Yet these changes were not mere drifting. In Cary's temperament a strong sense of social responsibility was frequently at odds with what he called 'something Baudelairean'. This quarrel with himself, out of which he was to make his most poetic novels, accounts for his growing restlessness and dissatisfaction as he moved from the free-and-easy life of an art student in France and Edinburgh to the equally free-and-easy life of an undergraduate who went to Oxford in order to talk and make friends, and thence to try his hand as a writer in Paris and London. The ennui which clouded his enthusiasm for the Bohemian life is sometimes plain in the diary he kept during the months when he shared a Paris studio with John Middleton Murry:

We took Miss B. to her studio in the Rue de Tounon. She would not go in, however, and said we all ought to do something foolish. M[urry] still trying to be amiable, turned eleven somersaults on the pavement. I watched with two two-foot loaves of Miss B.'s under my arm and Marguerite's programme, which she had left with me in my hand, not to crush it – and found it all very dull. However, I was too tired at this time to be sulky. So over the Seine and at length back by half-past two, Miss B. talking extraordinarily well. Biard shut, so to bed, very hungry, where I talked with M. till half past four before going to sleep.

The Balkan War of 1912–1913 offered Cary a temporary escape from this existence into one he felt to be more purposeful. With Gertrude Ogilvie's medical student brother, he served in a Red Cross unit attached to the Montenegrin Army. When the war came to an end, Cary once again sought a form of service, this time to the society in which he had been born. The Irish Land Act of 1881, in transferring land-ownership to peasant proprietors, had caused such Ascendancy families as the Joyces and the Carys to 'rot off the land', in Standish O'Grady's brutal phrase. Some members of the old landed class were able to adapt themselves to the new order. Notable among them was Sir Horace Plunkett, who had made it his life's work to improve the output of Irish smallholdings by the establishment of farmers' co-operatives, and had guided them, since the turn of the century, through his Department of Agricultural and Technical Instruction. Plunkett invited Cary to join this; and Cary leapt at an opportunity of returning to the land of his birth in work that would help to heal the old rift between the peasant Irish and the 'English Garrison' – most of whom, like the Carys themselves, had in fact been Irishmen since the reign of Elizabeth. But Plunkett's younger colleagues were not as ready as Plunkett himself to welcome back members of the dispossessed Ascendancy; and after a few weeks one of them bluntly told Cary that it had been decided not to employ graduates as such, but only men with a specialized knowledge of agriculture.

In 1913 the cry everywhere was for specialists. England was beginning to feel alarm at Germany's great technical advances. Colonial governors, however, notably the recently appointed

Governor of a unified Nigeria, Sir Frederick Lugard, continued to believe that the best administrators could be recruited from among the younger sons of the professional and landed classes, even if they possessed no special qualifications for the work. Encouraged by this, Cary applied for the Northern Nigerian Political Service. In point of fact, his post-school experience added up to very good qualifications. He had a degree in law; campaigning and medical experience in the Balkans; and administrative and agricultural experience in Ireland. It is not surprising that out of sixty-four applicants in the autumn of 1913, Cary was one of half a dozen selected.

In his choice of the Nigerian political service, as in his Montenegrin and Irish ventures, Cary was still seeking scope for the socially responsible side of his nature, just as he was to do many years after he had become a writer, by means of party political activities. He needed, perhaps to satisfy the strongly protective instinct often found in those who have been deprived of a parent; he had lost his mother when he was eight and his stepmother when he was fifteen. The instinct was too deepseated and powerful to be given direct expression; but in *A House of Children* he voices it through the thin mask of 'Evelyn Corner'.

> The teaching, too [at Evelyn's preparatory school], was little more worldly than that of a nurse, who, for her own sake, teaches the purest Christian unselfishness. It was mixed, of course, with patriotic and imperial sentiments; but all with stress upon duty and responsibility. To be an Englishman was to be born to a great destiny; as warrior and guardian of freedom and justice and peace. These doctrines became old-fashioned in the last twenty years, but Robert, and afterwards Harry and myself, breathed them as part of the atmosphere which entered into our very bones. . . . A lecture from a boy's parent, a sailor, about chasing slave dhows in the Gulf, went to the bottom of our feelings at one flash.
>
> Of course we heard nothing of the other side of the old Empire: the gold grabbers; the cotton lords of India; and we had no conception, for our masters had none, of a real freedom. Our idea, like theirs was abstract and legal, or romantic. We had no notion that poverty came into the question and was, with ignorance, the chief enemy of freedom.
>
> (p. 34)

Slave trading was still widely prevalent in Africa when Cary was a schoolboy. At the time Sir Frederick Lugard was appointed High Commissioner to Northern Nigeria in 1900, the horsemen of the powerful Fulani Emirs on the southern edge of the desert were still raiding the pagan tribes of the Middle Belt, slaughtering the unsaleable without mercy, and hawking the able-bodied in the market places of Kano and Sokoto. When in 1916 Cary himself trekked the whole extent of Northern Nigeria, from Nafada to Borgu, he once rode for half an hour across the empty space between two city gates. Grass-covered desolation was all that remained of a vast city which had been wiped out, not many years before, by the Emir of Kontagora, whom Cary knew (*Britain and West Africa*, p. 48). This was the Emir Ibrahim who, reproached by the British for his slave-raids, retorted with the question: 'Can a cat be stopped from mousing?' In *Castle Corner*, Cary reanimated the same desolate city with the horrors of a slave raid, drawing on first-hand accounts given him by Africans who had taken part in Lugard's 1903 expedition against the Northern Emirs.

This expedition brought the Emirates finally under Britain; but Lugard, in his policy of indirect rule, aimed at leaving the indigenous rulers as far as possible masters in their own domains. A Resident (the name was meant to suggest an ambassador) was appointed as counsellor to each Emir. Peace and justice were the first objectives: slave-raiding had to cease, though slavery as an institution was left to die a natural death; Moslem law prevailed in the native courts wherever it was held not to conflict with Western standards of justice. The Northern Emirs' courts in fact had considerable, sometimes even capital, powers; but in the pagan areas of the Plateau and of the Niger and Benue valleys, where Islam had not penetrated at the time of the British conquest, the powers of the newly-formed native courts were very circumscribed. All serious cases had to be tried by the British administrator. As Lugard, in his determination to make justice free to all, also barred professional lawyers from the courts, heavy juridical responsibility fell on men who often had scanty training for the work. By and large, however, it can be said that when, less than a dozen years after its original annexation, the Protectorate was amalgamated with the southern provinces, the administration was well on the way to achieving one kind of freedom for the Nigerian people: freedom from the fear of oppression and extortion.

This concept of freedom, as Cary indicates in the passage just quoted from *A House of Children*, was something quite different from that which began to prevail in the thirties and forties of this century. Freedom from want, as far as ever it entered colonial plans, was thought of as something that followed in due though slow course from the freedom from fear that the Pax Britannica provided; unharassed by tribal wars and slave raids, and by fiscal extortion, the people could be left to develop their natural resources in their own way. The bush officer's text was Kipling's 'Clear the land of evil, drive the road and bridge the ford'; his main duties, over and above the preservation of law and order, were the assessment of his district for tax, the collection of that tax (divided, in a developed Emirate, between the Native Treasury and the Central Treasury), the careful surveying of the area, and the building of communications through which trade could be improved. Health and education services were thought of, when they were thought of at all, as the final outcome of this policy of self-supported development. The 1912 Annual Report on Northern Nigeria, which Cary acquired when he was reading up the country preparatory to sailing in 1914, states blandly that 'The principle of providing the natives with a liberal education in a manner that will enable them to preserve, maintain and develop their national character, is being closely followed.' It then gives the total number of pupils at school, in a territory whose population numbered over ten millions, as two hundred and fifty. Not until the late nineteen-twenties was it realized that health and education are the beginning and not the end of development, since without them the will and ability to develop, which Cary came to consider the only true and positive freedom, could not exist.

But in 1914 neither Cary himself nor the other successful cadets in the Political Service were much troubled by the prospect of running an enormous country on a home-made shoe-string. They were drawn by the romance of Mungo Park's Niger and its wide tributaries; by the knowledge that they would themselves often be explorers, mapping for the first time the districts assigned to them. They were attracted, as the English always have been, by the dignity, independence and courage of the Moslem rulers and by the medieval pomp of their retinues; attracted also by the opportunity to win the confidence of Stone Age tribesmen living in clustered beehive huts on the shoulders of the Jos plateau.

Bauchi Province, where Cary had the good fortune to be posted, offered all this and more besides. It is the most beautiful of the northern provinces, some of it four thousand feet high with a climate more typical of the east than the west of Africa. Its high grasslands, as yet in Cary's day only slightly scarred by the workings of tin mines, are broken by small flat-topped hills like kopjes where it needs a sharp eye to distinguish the tribesmen's thatched huts and granaries from the giant boulders that give them protection. To the east the land falls away to a different landscape: the plains of Bauchi and the thin orchard bush that lies along the Gongola, a tributary of the Benue.

2

Although factual records of Joyce Cary's first tour in Nigeria are scanty, he left many near-factual impressions of it in the sketches, mostly unpublished, which he wrote about Evelyn Corner. The name is a recognizable variant of his own, with its ambiguous first part (he suffered a good deal from being called Miss Cary by reviewers) and its punning surname derived from his habit, when in Paris, of Gallicizing his name to Carré. One of these sketches describes Evelyn Corner's arrival in Bauchi. He gets as far as Zaria, on the main Northern railway, to be told that the special train arranged to take him up to the plateau on the miners' light railway is not likely to arrive for a day or two. The stationmaster and

Corner's servants all assume that he will camp on the platform; and just as he is about to protest at this unorthodox idea, Corner realizes its merits. The platform is dry and ant-proof, and wood and water are easily available. So he leaves matters to his household:

It turned out that the railway platform, as a home, had disadvantages. It was a place outside civilization where people were too careless or too anxious to trouble about each other. Naked pagans, with their tickets in their wool, would knock over Corner's chair, and trample over him in their fear of missing a train, or their anxiety to salute the stationmaster. Young clerks, going to their first official post, used his rug to wipe their patent leather shoes. The passengers of a local train coming in unexpectedly, while the young man was having his bath in a little ring of loads, would come to the windows to stare at him, and discuss his colour and shape and shout jokes at each other. But he was no more embarrassed than any other animal at the zoo. After three days on the platform he still felt that kind of elation, which belongs probably only to emperors or geniuses whose whole existence is on a lofty and separate plane, independent of conventions and ordinary barriers.

Finally the tank engine, drawing a single truck, arrives and carries Corner up before dawn onto the high plateau.

Dawn broke slowly, pale green and shewed a landskip which looked like scientific places of the moon, a wilderness of broken rocky hills, as green and bare as brittle glass. The truck was tilted at an absurd angle. It seemed like a flying carpet in the transformation scene. Then the sun came up and the hills were brown, rusty, barren, not at all like any romantic idea of Africa, but much better of course, because they were real.

('Railway Camp').

In actual fact, Cary made the journey in June 1914 in the company of two other newly recruited political officers. In a discarded preface to one of his African novels he vividly describes the moment when the train reached the end of the line, and the young men alighted to receive the acclaims of a crowd of pagans who rushed towards them, brandishing spears. As Cary and the two others stood against the truck's wheels, feeling astonished and embarrassed, 'the whole mob fell on their faces and threw dust on their heads. One of the servants who, in a cloth cap and singlet from Manchester, stood above us on the truck, folding up a chair, said in a contemptuous

voice, "Dey say you king of de world, sah." ' (N85). Both the story
and the memoir attempt to recapture the nervous tension of Cary's
first days in Nigeria and the way this tension sharpened his percep-
tions and responses; they convey very well Cary's bewilderment at
the unexpectedness of Africans who prostrated before him in one
place and walked over him in another, and his apprehension at
finding himself a junior in a new service. He knew himself to be a
raw recruit; no one actually in the service had much regard for the
three months' course of lectures on tropical diseases, tropical
products, criminal and Moslem law, accountancy and surveying
that he had attended at the Imperial Institute in South Kensington.
Although the surveying was to come in useful when Cary was alone
in Borgu, his real training was of the in-service kind, which he
received in the District Office at Bauchi.

The District Officer in charge of Bauchi Division, H. S. W.
Edwardes, was waiting at Naraguta to receive the newcomers. He
and Cary travelled on to Bauchi together, and in the course of the
journey Cary conceived an admiration and affection for Edwardes
which lasted the rest of his life. He tried several times to capture in
words the mood of that ride to Bauchi under the title of 'Too good
to be true', but he abandoned these attempts because he found he
could give only picturesque details about Edwardes himself – his
eccentricities of dress (he rode in enormous boots of an Elizabethan
buccaneering pattern), his gargantuan breakfasts at the morning
halt, his passion for Gibbon, whom he read aloud – but nothing of
the man's real nature. Edwardes, who had been in the country since
1905, was deeply committed to the Africans in his care. One small
sketch for a story, drawn up some years after Cary had left Nigeria,
evokes the kind of scene which occurred in the divisional office at
Bauchi whenever Edwardes felt the authorities were not treating his
people with the consideration they deserved:

> Bauchi. My people, report to the govnr. What do you think of the style.
> but sir, I don't think he'll like it. Gulard [Lugard] is a bit of an autocrat.
> E. blows up. killing my people *my* people.
>
>   (N63)

Edwardes was an enthusiast for education at a time when most administrators were content with what the Bauchi Provincial Report for 1914 calls 'a little simple education of pagans by the Church Missionary Society'. He started the Province's first school in 1915 and so increased the number receiving education (in an area larger than Scotland) from fifteen to eighty-two. Edwardes' other passion was road-building. He was the anonymous author of a pamphlet on the subject which became a best-seller in British colonies between the wars. As District Officers were not supposed to indulge themselves by building roads, which were a matter for the Public Works Department, he had to call it *The Improvement of Native Paths*. Rudbeck, in *Mister Johnson*, gets his enthusiasm for roads from 'Old Sturdee' the name under which Edwardes is disguised in Cary's published and unpublished writings; and a letter from Edwardes written after Cary had been wounded in the Cameroon Campaign in 1915 takes us straight into the world of *Mister Johnson*, where the bush officer waged continual war with the Secretariat:

> I am going to get some roads made this dry weather if it lands me in Stellenbosch. There is humour in the fact that the opposition to and distrust of any beneficent measure always comes from above. One has to fight the Government all the time. The man who is discouraged by rebuffs and snubs never gets anything done. I enjoy the battle and in the end they usually let me do it to shut me up.
>
> (22 September 1915)

At the time Cary was working in the Bauchi office to learn the administrative routine, Edwardes was actively engaged in measures to combat the famine which had followed a prolonged drought. When Cary travelled on in late July to Nafada in Gombe, the Province's most easterly district, his journey took him through the edge of the famine areas, and memories of the scenes he saw there were still painful to him nearly thirty years later when he wrote, 'No one in Europe seems to have any notion what famine is like, in the scale of suffering' (N85). The famine was followed, in the early months of 1915, by a smallpox outbreak in which Cary encountered

for the first time the strange resignation of people who have not yet
the knowledge that might enable them to fight calamity:

> I did not know what patience meant until I saw old men dying by the
> roadside, with dying children in their arms; or the smallpox camp where
> whole families sat all day, with their enormously swollen faces, waiting
> upon fate with a submission so complete that I had to have some of them
> spoon-fed. They had lost all confidence in remedy and even in food. I
> daresay they felt that the familiar corn might poison them. They were
> some of those millions who have died every year, in peace time, for
> countless thousands of years, in misery which no war could exaggerate,
> and they accepted their fortune in such patience that they did not even
> resent it. They did not dream of blaming anyone for it. They were
> perfectly good-natured and ready to be cheerful. They laughed at a joke,
> especially if they thought they were meant to be amused.
>
> But I realized then, that like children, they had no alternative. They
> were so completely ignorant and unable to help themselves, that their
> only defence against what seemed to them the cruel fantasies of chance
> and the mysterious injustice of nature, was resignation.
>
> (*A House of Children*, pp. 135-6)

At Nafada, Cary was to work under J. F. J. Fitzpatrick, learning
more about the duties of a District Officer, which Lugard, with nice
understatement, described as 'very varied':

> In an isolated station he may have to discharge the functions of all the
> departments – postal, customs, police and engineer – in addition to his
> normal work. He is the medium of communication between the military
> or the departmental officer and the native chiefs in matters of labour and
> supplies, and is especially charged to see that labourers are fully paid and
> properly treated. To him alike the missionary, the trader and the miner
> look for assistance and advice. The leper and the slave find in him a
> protector.
>
> (*The Dual Mandate*, p. 134)

As the 'normal work' included acting as magistrate, supervising
native courts, enforcing ordinances, issuing licences, keeping up
accounts and rendering prescribed returns; and as the District Officer
had to be careful not to let this routine work at headquarters prevent
him from travelling all over his district, administering justice,
settling disputes and collecting statistics, it is not surprising that

some of the individuals concerned were a little sardonic about
Lugard's Galahad concept of their mission. Fitzpatrick, a sharp-
tongued Irishman, was an outspoken critic of indirect rule, and his
post-war comments on it allegedly resulted in his being banished,
like Cary's Jim Latter, to an insalubrious station on the Lower
Benue. He had a healthy scorn for red tape and wrote breezy prose
that was at the furthest possible remove from gobbledegook.
Between 1914 and 1917 he contributed to *Blackwood's Magazine* a
number of sketches of Gombe and of the Cameroons, including a
briskly cynical account of the division as it was at the time of Cary's
arrival at the end of July.

> In the summer of 1914 Mr. Harris [Fitzpatrick himself] was administering
> with more or less success an area that we will call Gembo. It extended over
> some thousands of square miles and presented much physical variety.
> There were very rocky mountains and there were some very extensive
> tracts of swamp. Politically also Gembo was interesting – in that the rocky
> mountains were covered as to their tops by villages of pepper-pot-like
> huts full of naked and very active savages, whilst the flat parts of the
> division supported a population of slender, much-clothed Muslim farmers
> and cattle-owners. The hill-toppers would listen to no orders, and they
> flicked arrows at Augustus and his police escort when he went out to see
> them: the dressy people below listened to everything – and then went
> away and busied themselves devising means to defeat the purpose of the
> Political Officer.
>
> (Volume CC, p. 260)

The 'station' at Nafada consisted of a few bungalows by the
Gongola inhabited by two army officers, the doctor, the D.O., and
his assistant. Now that the rains had broken, carrying away the
telegraph line to Bauchi, dining-out was made virtually impossible
by the flood-water which surrounded each bungalow, and Cary,
for all his delight in this novel life, must have found Nafada a dull
place. It did not remain so. In a sketch, 'Marching as to War',
which comparison with a similar account by Fitzpatrick shows to be
largely factual, Cary describes the astonishment in the station one
day in August 1914 when a horseman galloped in with a bundle of
telegrams indicating that all the troops in Northern Nigeria were

marching on Nafada. The Englishmen decided the province must be in a state of revolt. The young A.D.O. with an eyeglass, recently arrived from Oxford, looked expectantly at the wide, sky-filled river and the empty landscape from which an occasional thin line of smoke arose. 'The young man stood feeling for rebellion in the air. He found it at once. He said in a voice of lively interest. "That's why there's no one about." ' But at this moment the D.O. appeared with the true explanation: Britain and Germany were at war, and all the units of the West African Frontier Force in the country were to be concentrated on key-points along the Cameroons frontier.

> Troops came streaming into Nafada [Fitzpatrick wrote] from three points of the compass, horse soldiers and foot soldiers, signallers, and doctors, machine guns and carriers, black soldiers, white officers, and small parties of Europeans – miners, traders, officials, – volunteers for the Cameroons Expeditionary Force. From Kano and Bauchi and Katagum and Naraguta and Pankshin they came, hundred of miles, through swamps and across rivers and over mountains, all hurrying to the front. The two notable things in Nafada at the time were a famine and an unfordable river, half a mile wide, full of brown, rushing, ugly-looking water. All arrivals had to be fed, and had to be got across the river, and things hummed in Nafada for some weeks.

> (*Blackwood's Magazine*, CCI, pp. 250-1)

Fitzpatrick sent Cary upstream to organize a transit camp, buy grain and meat from the surrounding villages, assemble all available canoes for a temporary ferry over the Gongola and recruit such veterans of Lugard's campaigns as he could find. Jottings for a story he meant to base on this assignment capture Cary's mood at the time. 'Toils and enjoys it. All because of an idea. So do the soldiers. But the natives have a different idea of things and don't want to give grain' (N85). As people were dying of starvation in villages not very far away, this reluctance was understandable. Matters were made worse when the troops simply took grain without the villagers' consent; and before long Fitzpatrick, who sent daily runners out from Nafada with letters containing light-hearted comments on the personnel of the whole province and their reactions to the emergency, had to report that Edwardes was extremely angry with the way the troops were behaving towards 'his people' in Gombe. Cary, in some distress, hurried off apologies and an offer to seek out a wronged village with compensation and received in reply a warm-hearted letter: 'Go ahead, my dear fellow, and compensate any of my people oppressed by the military' (2 September 1914). The same letter contained the news that T. F. Carlyle, who was to relieve Fitzpatrick at Nafada, was on the road. Fitzpatrick too had heard from Carlyle (the wire was now repaired) that he wanted post-horses to be ready for him all along the route. 'Well Nafada didn't want saving – and this isn't Ghent – besides, if it were there's no good news to bring. So I wired Carlyle no horses available – and now he's going to start today or tomorrow and come along like an ordinary person' (19 August 1914).

By the time Carlyle arrived, Cary had returned to Nafada, since all the troops had passed through. Although Carlyle did not gallop up post-haste, he made a profound impression on Cary; so profound that he was to haunt his imagination as a writer for years to come. Another District Officer with whom Cary once spent a single night in the bush was able to recall, nearly fifty years later, the enthusiasm with which Cary had talked about Carlyle. He made a similar impression on everyone who served with him. A contemporary writes: 'Carlyle was a huge man, with large ideas – everything about him was big. He built enormous mud houses, made prodigious journeys in his district, and was in every way a forceful character. He never hesitated in a decision, and having made it he stuck to it, and the people liked that.' (E. L. Mort).

Carlyle was as deeply committed to his work as Edwardes, though in a different way. He was what was known as 'a pagan man'. Profoundly interested in the people of the province and their traditions (he had spent most of his 1914 leave writing a history of Gombe), he had for the past eight years worked to gain the confidence of the pagan tribes, who, driven back to the hills by the Moslem invaders, regarded all strangers with hostile suspicion and were apt to greet them with, at the least, a few beehives tipped down the rocks, and at the most with a shower of poisoned arrows. Like every pagan man, he had his favourite tribe, the Tangale, regarded by every other administrator in the Province (according to Cary) as 'low scoundrels'. Carlyle went amongst them without hesitation. Even an official document describes him as 'notorious for his personal courage'.

Carlyle was a brilliant talker as well as a man of action. But there were few opportunities for Cary to enjoy his talk during this tour, since Carlyle was soon off on a visit to the low scoundrels, who had taken the opportunity of the outbreak of war and the rumoured withdrawal of all troops to eat a Hausa trader. Fitzpatrick had also left. He characteristically rode off to the Cameroons Campaign with a small boy (called 'Mister Johnson') whom he had adopted and who refused to be left in any place of safety, and with a select library of English and French literature. He then distinguished himself equally characteristically by taking over the command of the stronghold of Gurin and repulsing a prolonged German attack at a time when he was still technically a civilian. Cary was meanwhile left alone in Nafada, where he soon had an opportunity to use the medical experience he had gained in Montenegro. An invalided political officer travelling through Gombe went down with blackwater fever and – to quote the official report – 'it was only through the general efficiency of Mr. Cary, Assistant District Officer, acting on instructions telegraphically communicated by Dr. Moiser, that his life was saved'.

It may have been after the doctor's arrival in December that Cary made the acquaintance of another pagan man, named Jimmy Finch, whom he was to describe in an article called 'Christmas in Africa' and also to draw upon for the character of Jim Latter. Finch had imported a pack of beagles from England as a way of assisting his tribesmen to get more and better 'beef', of which there is never enough in West Africa. He presided as M.F.H. in beautiful boots and a velvet cap, mounted, and holding over his head a large striped umbrella inscribed 'Stolen from J. Finch':

> Both he and they loved hunting and he made the hunt for them. . . . It was under that immense prestige, the discipline of the Master of Fox Hounds, that stray tin-prospectors were reasonably safe from murder and

missionaries could preach, and even the telegraph wire (much valued for bangles, anklets, etc.: every good husband was expected to provide it) was left uninterrupted for as much as three months at a time.

After Christmas, Cary was once again in the bush, arranging for the transit of troops; the siege of Mora Mountain in the north had been raised, and French and British troops were converging on the upper Benue valley, preparatory to an attack on Garua. Cary himself was on the reserve of officers, on the strength of his Montenegrin experience. By late April he was at Yola, the British military headquarters, attached to H Infantry Company, Second Battalion, Nigeria Regiment.

3

If the chivalric ideals of a latter-day Imperialism were still represented in the Political Service at the time Cary went to Nigeria, the worst aspect of nineteenth-century Imperialism, its arbitrary partition of Africa, bore bitter fruit in the Cameroons campaign of 1914 to 1916. British and German administrators on each side of the long frontier extending from the Bight of Benin to Lake Chad had always been on excellent terms. Now they found themselves forced into a meaningless enmity. Things were a thousand times worse for their African subjects, some of whose tribes were cut in two by a boundary drawn in a Berlin office and for whom British and Germans were barely distinguishable from each other. All historians of the campaign marvel that the Nigerian soldier should have fought so well when the issues at stake meant nothing to him.

The 'Soldiering Sketches' – finished, half-finished or merely outlined – which survive among Joyce Cary's papers show that the political issues of the campaign also concerned him very little. The experience he sought to preserve in these sketches was above all the Conradian one of self-discovery through novel situations and actions: the kind of incident described in a published story, 'Bush River', in which Corner takes a risk which is for once justifiable if not in fact justified – the guide has not appeared and his men are on the verge of panic – of swimming his pony across a river in spate.

In his delight at his pony's grace and strength, Corner does not even hear the sergeant's warning that there are Germans on the opposite bank. It is only when he and Satan are across and he is lying exhausted on the ground that he sees the outline of a German soldier's cap and rifle barrel:

> He hadn't even a revolver, so he lay quite still, fatalistic, but not resigned. For he was resentful. He detested this monster of his own stupidity.
> At the same time he was in great terror, the calm, helpless terror of the condemned. He was holding his breath for the shot. He had a queer sensation so vivid that he still remembered it twenty-years after, of floating lightly off the ground.
>
> (*Spring Song*, p. 17)

This kind of campaigning, in which for days on end Cary led a small detachment of Nigerian soldiers through the bush, brought him into close contact with Africans for the first time. He even found himself thinking in Hausa. Sometimes he and his men were bedfellows, as on the wet night described in another story, 'Umaru', when their only shelter was a tent fly spread over them to give the effect of 'a vast family bed with one white and nineteen black faces sticking out all round a large patchwork quilt'. Cary, wakeful, and elated by the wild sky overhead, begins to talk to the old Hausa sergeant lying beside him. As the differences between them, which are the differences between age and youth, black and white, Moslem and Protestant, define themselves more and more sharply in their talk, the sense of intuitive sympathy grows warmer in Cary's mind. The Coleridgean storm setting helps to make the story a striking account of the way the creative imagination works, penetrating and yet preserving the individuality of other minds.

The difficult fighting conditions described in 'Umaru' prevailed everywhere in the Northern Cameroons during the wet season of 1915. It was impossible to maintain communications across flooded rivers and through elephant grass ten feet high, along a line four hundred miles long. In Cary's own words, the war was one of 'raids, ambushes, sieges, enormous marches, and especially surprises. . . . Whole columns would disappear for weeks together, to burst out, a thousand miles away, upon a panic-stricken capital. Two patrols would stumble upon each other by accident in high jungle and stare with amazement for a few seconds before grabbing their rifles' (*Spring Song*, p. 11). The effect on the nerves of this kind of warfare is caught in an unpublished story called 'The Raft', which is the account of an actual incident. Cary and thirty Nigerian soldiers were clearing a path for a large gun, when they reached a river in spate. Cary ordered the men to cut wood for a raft, and nicked some suitable young trees for the purpose. They went to work with shouts of laughter that could easily have been heard by any German detachment in the neighbourhood.

'I say, Corporal, we don't want to make too much noise, you know.'

'No, sir.' The Corporal's face twisted, and all at once a man behind was seized with giggles. At once the whole party exploded with loud giggles, squeaks, heehaws.

The Corporal began to reprove them, but burst into a neigh of laughter right in the face of the young officer. Corner was disconcerted, but he thought, 'After all, it's a good thing they're not worried.' He therefore smiled upon them as if to say.'Be happy, my children.'

At this the men became almost hysterical. One young recruit made sounds like whooping-cough and bent down till his woolly green cap fell right off.

Luckily Corner's breakfast was ready. He was able to withdraw with dignity. With dignity, good nature returned to him, and after breakfast, he thought, 'Really, they're nice chaps – it's not their war – and here they are, laughing away.'

He went again to the pickets. The noise of laughter pursued him. It seemed very loud. Then there was an explosion like a gun which brought the young man up short. Machine-guns rattled, another field gun cracked; there was a loud, rushing sound; Corner suddenly perceived that what he was listening to was only the fall of a tree.

But the noise must be audible for miles. He stood, still holding his breath, and listening. Suddenly he heard the Germans; the scrape of feet on hard ground, a quick rustle, the unmistakable sound of soldiers running from one cover to another. He dropped behind a bush and pulled out his Webley. The chopping and laughter, from fifty yards away, sounded, in the dead stillness of a tropical midday, like a firework show. The young man, crouching, raced towards a picket, twisting and turning. The men on picket were not laughing. They received him with looks of horror. Their faces said, 'We're done for.'

Corner, however, having got his breath, simply warned them to look out and went on to the next picket. In half an hour he was back at the main body, exhausted, soaked in sweat, but recovered from his panic. First of all he had got used to it, and then it had simply evaporated. The men were still chopping and giggling, but in a languid manner. The ramp was finished, and a pile of logs lay ready at the water's edge. It was very hot. The big trees that were left looked like dirty metal and the green shade smelt like a marquee. Corner told the choppers to lay off and rest; and sent a party to gather creepers to tie the raft together. Then he lit his pipe and drew out an envelope to plan the details of the raft.

Completely relaxed again, Cary was soon asleep; but he was wakened by an alarm that sent the whole party manœuvring for an attack on a party of Germans who had marched into the camp from the north. After an hour of high tension, the Germans proved to be Cary's own sergeant and his party, who seemed no less amused than the others at the idea of the raft. In some exasperation, Cary told them to put the first log in the water. They did so and it immediately sank out of sight. The trees were ironwood. That was the joke.

Although this incident was one of Cary's most vivid recollections of the Cameroons campaign, he did not publish it. The themes that his jottings show he wanted it to carry – '*Forgetfulness* of danger and the terror of *realisation afterwards*. War as a succession of idle moods' – were more easily developed in 'Bush River'; the story of the soldiers' amusement at Cary's mistake, while it was a good campaign yarn, got in the way of the theme, and Cary showed sound judgement in preserving the one story in print and leaving the other in manuscript. But 'The Raft' is a lively autobiographical piece, conveying well the hour-to-hour fluctuations in active service between taut anxiety and relaxed idleness. The strain of such fighting conditions was great. Cary made it the subject of a bitter story about an honest young officer who admitted to having panicked at the threat of an ambush, and who was in consequence dubbed 'Guda' – the Hausa for 'runaway'. His self-esteem was undermined and he finally went to pieces; while one of his mockers, who behaved in exactly the same way on a subsequent occasion, brazened out the episode and went on to distinguish himself in the campaign. The story reflects the fascination Cary was to find, all through his life as a writer, in the blusterer, who could talk his way out of any situation: characters like Bonser in *A Fearful Joy*, who would never acknowledge the gap between what they really were and what they fancied themselves to be.

Cary's company was involved in three major actions in the course of the war. All three were attacks on German mountain strongholds. The first, against Garua, which fell in June 1915, was more in the nature of a siege than a battle, and the garrison capitulated chiefly because its supplies had run out. Cary's adventures as escort to the French field-gun, which are described in 'The Raft' and 'Bush River', presumably occurred on the long march between Garua and the northern fortress of Mora Mountain, which General Cunliffe's force attacked in September. Mora was a formidable stronghold. The attack had to be made in mist and darkness by climbing down a deep ravine, between boulders where it was impossible to see one's footing, and then scrambling up the steep slopes of the mountain itself, under constant fire from the German breastworks. At the second attempt, Cary's company got within sixty yards of the German positions, but food and water could not be got to them, and finally they were forced to withdraw. The huge rocks on the mountain were of course a protection as well as a hazard; Cary owed his life to the fact that he was almost entirely covered by one when he was sniped at by the enemy. Many years later he startled an interviewer by remarking, 'I was killed in the first war':

> I got a bullet that scraped my mastoid, and of course it felt as if my brains were blown to pieces, and knocked me right out. And I just sat down to think: Well, this is it, and it is easy.   (*Tamarack Review*, Spring, 1957)

And in a letter to his wife eighteen months after the occurrence he recalled that he 'had no unhappy thoughts or pain or fear – only a sort of surprise that such a terrible thing as death should happen so easily and suddenly' (2 March 1917).

The wound in fact did not prove serious; and after treatment at Yola, Cary was able to join his company on its long march to the south – four hundred and forty miles in five weeks – where they were to co-operate with the British and French in the Southern Cameroons in dislodging the Germans from the central plateau. Later, in criticizing the sentimental primitivism which was so often made a barrier to African development, Cary claimed that he knew what Rousseau's life according to nature was like: he had lived it on that march.

> In the war I lived for a time a perfectly healthy life – marching twenty-five miles a day, eating corn bread, almost raw meat, quantities of fruit. I was almost completely happy, that is to say, almost completely an animal. I did not think, or reflect. I felt well, brisk in the morning, tired at night. I slept as soon as I closed my eyes, and waked at the rustle of a leaf. I can't remember that I ever laughed or smiled, and I walked through blood on the road (the blood of some fellow shot in the advance action) without interest of any kind, or any emotion that I can remember. I was then almost a natural man. I met other natural men, black men, here and there, fine healthy fellows.
>
> But it took all day to keep me natural. When we had a short march once or twice, and camped early, I was sure to have a stomach ache and a feeling of lassitude in the evening, while my brain would recover enough activity to wonder where we were marching to, or when we would have more parcels of eatables; to enjoy conversation, and feel compassion for others, the men and the beasts, my own poor pony; sometimes even to enjoy a joke.

> (Borgu diary)

Cunliffe's objective was another mountain fortress, Banyo, a thousand feet above the plain and perhaps the most well-guarded and well-provisioned of all the German strongholds. The assault resembled that on Mora, with the infantry, including H Company, working its way up painfully for two days over rocks and through thorn scrub and long grass; but a larger and better co-ordinated force succeeded where the Mora attackers had failed, and after forty-eight hours they reached the summit, only to find that the German garrison had relinquished the fort and made their escape down the mountain through head-high grass and under cover of a storm.

This was the last major engagement Cunliffe's force had with the enemy. Cary's company was sent on to Fumban and then to Ngombe, where they lost touch with the retreating Germans. Cary himself was back in Yola for Christmas; by then the initiative had passed to the southern force who, by their capture of Yaounde, the Cameroons capital, brought the campaign to an end in January 1916.

Cary had by this date been in the country for longer than the usual tour of duty, and had spent nine months of that time soldiering in difficult terrain and in constant expectation of being ambushed. His wound from the Mora attack probably needed more attention than it had received, and he had been ill after the capture of Banyo. By his own account he was 'in a bad way at that time and a nervous wreck'. This exhaustion explains an incident of February 1916 which might be said to have had a long-lasting effect. Cary lost his temper with a group of men – presumably carriers – and 'knocked and kicked about freely'. An idiotic joker afterwards told him he had killed one of the men. Actually, no one was even hurt; but the experience of thinking he had murdered was every bit as traumatic as the moment at Mora when Cary thought he had himself been killed. It is possible that these two incidents, not far apart in time, may account for the way the surprise of the killer is linked with the surprise of the killed in *Mister Johnson* and *The Horse's Mouth*, and for the fact that Cary's two richest and most fully realised characters, Johnson and Jimson, are both technically guilty of murder.

The curious thing about these two episodes in the novels is that while Johnson's violence is wholly in keeping with Cary's intentions in *Mister Johnson*, Gulley's murder of Sara makes the reader un-comfortable as at a sudden imaginative failure. Johnson's action accords with his youth, nature and environment; we have been carefully prepared for it by his previous armed housebreaking; and it is essential to the plot. Gulley giving Sara a tap with the iron duke is as 'wrong' as the phrase itself, and its wrongness cannot be accounted for only by saying that the first person narrative forces Gulley to be unconvincingly explicit about a movement of blind rage and panic. The episode is wrong because it does not arise from the needs of the story; and dangerous as it is to establish a direct connexion between a novelist's actual experiences and what happens to his characters, it may very tentatively be suggested that the scene owes its origin to some fragment of undigested experience. If the experience belonged to 1916, Cary's outburst left him with a more serious wound than the one he received at Mora.

Gombe and Borgu
1916 – 1918

I

Joyce Cary and Gertrude Ogilvie were married in June 1916, during Cary's first leave from Nigeria. The day he left England two months later, Cary began a series of journal-letters to his wife which constitute a detailed record of his two remaining tours of duty in Africa. The only gaps in their sequence were those caused by the sinking of two mail ships in 1917. Rudbeck's difficulties with this kind of correspondence ('Having just written, "Today rather a funny thing happened," he is tapping his teeth trying to remember something that happened on Friday last') never troubled Cary; he was an exceptionally fluent writer, whose pen moved almost at the rate of his mind. His letters are thus an outstandingly vivid and immediate account, interrupted by six months' leave in England in 1918, of the next three years of his life.

Cary's first orders were to proceed to Lokoja, at the confluence of the Niger and the Benue. He travelled up-country by train and then down the Niger by the *Black Swan*. This river steamer figures in *An American Visitor*, where Cary recaptures the pleasure he always felt at being on water and especially at being on the Niger, a 'strong, brown god' among rivers. In his letters, his homesickness melts away in enjoyment of the voyage: 'We've run aground. Look at what happened to the "darling" I was writing. Everyone is yelling like blazes and ringing the bell. After all this life has interest. It is wonderful outside. Rain, lightning, the dark river roaring along, and all the compressed excited life on this little boat' (28 August 1916).

The boat reached Lokoja the next day; here Cary, who had expected to go on to headquarters at Yola, found he was to stay where he was for the present. The busy river port, which had a longer history of European contacts than most places in Nigeria (it is the Borrioboola-Gha of Mrs. Jellyby in *Bleak House*), left a deep enough impression on Cary, in the three weeks he was there, for him to make it the setting of *The African Witch*. Perhaps it stamped itself on his memory because it was the place where he began writing again after a silence of four years. He had attempted almost nothing since the novel of student life in Paris which Middleton Murry remembered him writing in their shared lodging. Now, in the middle of September 1916, he reported that he was becoming 'quite excited' with a story. Three days later he got his posting: not East Africa, as he had expected, but his old station of Nafada, where he was to command a company.

Nafada was three weeks' journey away from Lokoja, by river, rail and bush track. First Cary went back up the Niger as far as Baro, this time in a small boat. The cooking was done aft while Cary sat contentedly amidships, writing four thousand words a day. Like all Europeans, he was fair game for the curious:

> This morning, when I was exercising in nothing at all, I was startled by loud feminine squeaks and turned to see a whole small population, mostly ladies, watching me from ten yards' distance. I expect they thought my movements were religious. These little villages are so hidden among the trees we come on them in a minute as we wander along over the floods.
>
> (22 September 1916)

At Baro, the railhead, Cary found he had just missed a train, and another was not due for three days: 'This is not Willesden.' Actually, he was glad to have more time for the novel, of which the first draft was already finished. He now began to re-write, wrestling pleasurably with the difficulties of a first-person narrative – difficulties he did not brave in print until he was a very experienced novelist with half a dozen published books to his credit.

> That I of the book is not at all the I of me as you can understand. It is a fascinating amusement and I believe makes the most absorbing hobby in

the world – my hours fly away, I don't get into mischief, and I am happy all the time.

And later the same day –

I'm back on the verandah at my table with a whiskey soda at my elbow, a pile of lovely foolscap, a pipe and baccy and I'm whistling like a bird all for good spirits and gratitude for the lovely world. The sun is going down in glory, the river is steel inlaid with gold, the sky is blue and silver and saffron. . . .

(24 September 1916)

As before, Cary travelled by the main line to Zaria and then up to the plateau on the miners' light railway. This had been extended in the last two years, but Cary got no further on it than Jos, where the line had been washed away. Here he had to assemble his loads and find carriers. Sixty men were required to transport his basic furniture, personal possessions and a great number of food-boxes the two hundred odd miles to Nafada. They made a long procession which it was not easy to keep under control on the narrow bush tracks between high grass. The carriers' favourite trick was to get well ahead and eat up the market; that is, extort food without payment from the roadside vendors. But Cary, fitter and much happier than he had been at the beginning of the year, was able to cope with such situations without ill feeling on either side. An incident on the road helped to raise his prestige among his retinue. The inhabitants of a village mistook Cary for a very important person indeed, and turned out *en masse* to prostrate in his honour, until even the carriers felt compelled to do the same. Cary was a good deal more conscientious than most European travellers of the time in seeing that his carriers got regular meals and rests; and he never ceased to admire the way they could sing and joke their way over rough mountain paths in pitch darkness with sixty-pound loads on their heads.

Cary enjoyed the march. A start was made before dawn each day, and soon after daybreak he would pick out a large tree by a stream as a suitable bivouac. Table and chair were set up under the tree and a fire lighted for breakfast. After an hour or so the whole party, refreshed and rested, would move on a few more miles to camp at a bush resthouse – a thatched mud hut kept for the officer on tour – before the sun became intolerably high. The rest of the day was Cary's own, for writing. The novel was 'going famously' – 'all the characters blossoming and getting some flesh on their skeletons'. The almost Oriental contentment of some verses he wrote about this time shows Cary's relish for this mode of travel:

> Dawn comes up like a ray through the sea
> The trees stand up dark and still as memories
> I tread out the minutes of the present and look beyond.
> Far ahead is the cook with the kitchen-box
> Far behind the flute of the carriers
> When the run climbs I shall call for my pony,
> And when I reach camp, breakfast will be ready
> There under the thatch I shall smoke and feel satisfaction.

2

One reason why Cary enjoyed the march to Nafada so much was that he was looking forward to being back in his old station. But when he arrived he felt disappointed. Carlyle was on leave, and although the doctor was an old friend, the European group on the station was small and rather dull. There hung over the place some of the air of stagnation described in the posthumously published story, 'A Touch of Genius'. It was in any case a miasmal time of the year, when only the mosquitoes were happy. Cary caught dengue and in the profound depression which follows that fever he scrapped his novel 'because it wasn't good enough'. 'What ups and downs I have', he added, 'I suppose it's Irish blood' (7 December 1916). Cary's routine military duties could absorb only a fraction of his energies. He tried to rear a baby antelope, but it died. He read all the books in the station – mostly Thackeray – and sent desperate appeals home for more. Unless he had plenty to read, he found himself unable to write.

Carlyle returned in December. He was given a triumphal entry by the Emir, who went out to meet him with all his horsemen and rode in with him to an accompaniment of drums, ten-foot trumpets and bagpipes. He was soon off on tour to investigate the recent misdeeds of his Tangale. But his presence in the division rallied Cary out of his post-dengue gloom, and with the end of the rains his life fell into an agreeable pattern. Even the military duties had their lively moments, such as the time a dangerously violent labourer from the garrison charged into Cary's house. Cary, having sent for a file of men from the guard, tried to read a book and pretend the man did not exist – 'rather difficult as he was waving the spade and yelling a yard from me. You see I couldn't hit him, because that's against the rules and a bad thing in any case, and there was no one to arrest him on the spot, and he hadn't the sense to listen to an order. He laid all the guard out when they arrived and broke the corporal's head' (15 December 1916). The presence of a great number of soldiers' wives in the barracks brought hostilities quite as fierce, and much more explicit, than those of the mixed expatriate communities Cary had observed at Zaria and Naraguta: for example, the case 'all about three chickens and two women, and acting lance corporal Garuba Yola and Pte Garuba Maigumeri, and who killed the chicken and whose it was and which wife hit the other first, and if fourpence was a fair compensation for the chicken' (13 November 1916). Matters were complicated by the fact that many of the women in the barracks were the wives of men away fighting in East Africa. Their misdemeanours led Cary to embark on 'a great feminist experiment'.

Last week I appointed a Serikin Mata, or queen of the women to look after them. Yesterday after the ordinary orderly room was over, and defaulters marched off – in came the Ser. Mata – a tall stately lady in a blue robe followed by a fierce little woman carrying a large stick scowling ferociously – then two prisoners looking highly pleased with themselves – and then another policewoman with a stick and a scowl. The case was conducted with great solemnity – and the police were exceedingly officious about the etiquette of the court – wanting to knock the prisoners down whenever they opened their mouths. One lady was convicted of fighting, the other of loose behaviour in town, and they were both admonished – and warned that they will sit in the stocks at the next offence. The Serikin Mata has really shown herself most capable – chose her own police – states a case clearly, and is keeping a very unruly crowd of exceedingly unscrupulous women in excellent order. The police take themselves very seriously – they are both rather pretty young ladies but their scowls are terrible to witness when they guard the prisoner and their tones awfully fierce when they admonish her not to shout or pull her clothes off. One lady this morning calmly undressed herself during the case – I suppose to shew her indifference to the proceedings – she was up for violent assault and battery – and then put on her robes again with the most affected care – to the scandal of the whole court – I didn't laugh till they were outside again – one must look solemn on these occasions, – then I laughed so much I dropped my eyeglass.

(16 February 1917)

Cary's typical day at Nafada at this time was 'some solid work in the morning, a little writing after lunch, more work after tea, a rattling game of polo and a lazy hour in an easy chair with a pipe and a glass' (2 January 1917). But the writing was not going well and Cary could not get started on a second novel. A favourable review of Middleton Murry's first book left him restless and regretful that he had not himself settled down as a professional writer after the Montenegrin interlude.

Polo was a daily event at Nafada, thanks to Cary's tireless enthusiasm for the game. He managed to organize three-a-side play; there were four Europeans available, and Cary translated the rules into Hausa for the two Nigerian players, the court messenger and the Emir's secretary. The games were exciting, though not quite so packed with incident as the one described in *The African Witch*, which in fact brings together in three chukkas all the most memorable personalities and events of Nafada's dusty parade ground: Cary's own prized black pony, which bit all the other horses and most of the players; the excitable colour-sergeant who rode over the ball, causing the other players to gather round while their stallions reared and fought; the well-meaning young A.D.O. who was persuaded to learn to ride by playing polo; the visiting officer who 'could only ride in a riding school sort of way – thinking of himself and his pony the whole time', and who was indignantly surprised when the game did not stop because he had fallen. But as Cary pointed out many years later, in 'The Most Exciting Sport in the World', the local players could not lose face before their supporters by refusing to remount: 'O.C. troops among pagans has to be unbreakable and unkillable, he has to have the most powerful kind of juju or some local juju man will run his company.'

A comparison of Cary's letters and the article just quoted with *An African Witch* confirms that Cary meant Rackham in the novel to be something of a portrait of himself as he was in these Army days – 'an extremely conventional young officer, a little bit of a dandy'. Cary's dismissal of Middleton Murry's novel as 'just the sort of thing I should have expected from him – confused sex relations, neurotic love-affairs – and a great anxiety for originality at all costs' accords with this kind of personality. So does his anxiety over 'face'. A letter to his wife about an administrative muddle which occurred about this time, causing Cary's second-in-command to be promoted over his head (the error was quickly rectified), might have been written by Rackham himself: 'Out here . . . the position of every white man, sometimes his life, depends on his caste, his prestige. After all its only our prestige that keeps these millions of black men in order at all. . . . Prestige is important to every white man in Nigeria, so important there are a thousand rules made to support it that are not needed in more civilised places' (25 November 1916). Cary was to jump right out of the skin of this personality before he left Nigeria; and, looking back many years later at his Nafada self, he saw this jealousy for prestige in a historical light, as the root cause of the failure in race relations which caused so much frustration and unhappiness to black and white between the wars.

The Scotch Club in *The African Witch* derives, like the polo, from Cary's memories of evenings at Nafada, when the Englishmen on the station would gather for an hour or two of drinks and talk before dinner. 'Add the dark, trees and huts, the moon low down, some stars, a campfire, the table covered with bottles and glasses and four men in shirts, slacks and long boots lying in deck-chairs with pipes in their mouths, four or five mongrel dogs lying round, and a horse or two standing behind, and the river in front, and you have a picture of a small chop party' (10 December 1916). The talk was mainly shop; it ranged over laws, taxes, patrols, murderers, cattle, horses, small wars, chiefs, the customs of different tribes. When Carlyle was in the station he contributed his share of information about his cannibals, but he also widened the talk to include 'Providence and foreknowledge, will and fate': 'He is a wild kind of talker – he sees a notion like a butterfly – you can even notice his first glimpse of it fluttering, his eye lights up, and he is off at once and doesn't in the least mind where the chase ends – tonight he landed in some very deep ditches and thick thorns, but scarcely observed it in the excitement of the pursuit' (20 December 1916).

Cary was beginning really to enjoy Nafada again when he was restored to civil duties and moved to Kontagora, the most westerly province of Northern Nigeria and five weeks' journey from Gombe. He was given a ceremonial departure which he never forgot. The guard turned out and the buglers played the 'Hausa Farewell'.

The journey to Kontagora was a trying one. Cary was expecting news of the birth of his first child and was afraid that he would miss a telegram through being on the move. He was also angered by the fact that although he was going to do a D.O.'s work he would continue to receive an Assistant District Officer's pay of a little over three hundred pounds a year. And the weather was exhausting. It was the hottest time of the year for travel, with daytime temperatures well over a hundred Fahrenheit, and hot nights rendered sleepless by the fact that rest-houses were often in the middle of a village. Like all Europeans, Cary found the African tolerance of noise incomprehensible. His sense of isolation on the long, hot trek to a new post grew as he realised the loneliness of the Europeans on the stations he passed through. At Bauchi he found the District

Officer seriously ill with fever and nursed him until a doctor arrived
to take him to Naraguta. And at Naraguta he had the task of packing
up the personal possessions of an Englishman who had just died of
fever. So when he finally heard of his son's birth, his pleasure at the
news only sharpened the pain of separation. He was in the habit of
enclosing verses in his letters to his wife, and a few weeks after the
birth he sent her a very Blakean lullaby which is a distillation of all
the anxiety and loneliness he felt at this time:

> Sleep, sweeting, sleep
> Upon your mother's breast.
> That was my pillow too
> Where I could rest.
>
> I paid my heart
> For leave to lay me there.
> You paid with pain
> And cruelty did not spare.
>
> You wiser are
> And women's heart could read;
> Giving to those who take
> And not who need.

From Naraguta trains speeded up Cary's journey to Zunguru, and
he was at Kontagora by the end of April. Here he learnt from the
Resident that he was to reopen the former division of Borgu on the
Dahomey frontier.

3

'I don't like this part of the world' was Cary's first verdict on
Kontagora province. He was in Yelwa at the time, waiting for a
police escort to accompany him into Borgu. Meanwhile he suffered
from the sticky heat of the Niger valley at the beginning of the
rains, from the lack of letters about his son and from anxiety over
the war news: the Russian Revolution had just deprived the British
and French of a valuable ally. At last the police escort arrived. It

consisted of three men, two of whom were lame with guinea-worm. This was symptomatic of the difficulties Cary was to encounter in the next few months.

Borgu was at that time the most backward part of Nigeria. It is a long wedge of country between the Niger and the Dahomeyan frontier; so Cary's fluent French came in useful when he had to negotiate with the administrators on the other side of the frontier for the return of runaway highway robbers. Highwaymen did well in the division, because an important trade route to Sokoto and Timbuctoo ran through it, but nobody else was particularly prosperous. The population was sparse, probably fewer than forty thousand in an area of twelve thousand square miles. The district was ruled by two minor Emirs, one at Bussa beside the Niger rapids in which Mungo Park had drowned and the other in more hilly and healthy country at Kaiama, and by a number of village heads on the Dahomey trade route. A pagan tribe, the Gungawa, lived in the swampy Agwarra wastes to the north of the division, which even now can be visited only on horseback or by boat. Today the Gungawa bring their produce by canoe to the market at New Bussa, looking very much like the Birri in *An American Visitor*, for whom they were probably one model. Those parts of the division which are not swamp are featureless orchard bush, a form of vegetation which has none of the appeal of the luxuriant southern forests or the wide northern plains; a rolling countryside broken by occasional rocky hills is dotted over with small trees, stunted from the bush fires by which the farmers clear and fertilize their plots every dry season, leaving the landscape blackened and desolate.

Borgu had been in the English news in 1897 at the time of Lugard's march on Nikki. Lugard had been helped in this enterprise by the Emir of Kaiama, who was to remain his loyal friend until his death in 1912. After that, everything went wrong in Borgu. Both the reigning Emirs were unwisely deposed and an equally unwise choice made of their successors. As there was no British officer at the time in the division, which was administered from Yelwa on the far side of the Niger, these new rulers were given an unusually free hand for extortion and oppression. The result was a popular rising a few months before Cary's arrival. A capable political officer who had been in the division before 1912 was sent to turn out the worst offenders; and later in 1917 it was decided to make Borgu a division of Kontagora Province and to station Joyce Cary at Kaiama as the officer in charge.

Cary himself was well aware of the difficulties of this assignment. 'I shall go for bush on Monday – I don't know what is in store for me but I foresee a rough time – I shall be lord of some 10,000 square miles, mostly deserted bush, with a large population of lions snakes crocodiles and mosquitoes – the administration is in confusion and the people backward' (5 May 1917). He was on his own in Borgu for the next seven months. In the days before refrigeration and motor transport this meant living, in Cary's phrase, 'worse than a navvy'. He was sometimes without wheat flour for weeks on end. Meals were unvaryingly yam and chicken, unless Cary broke into his small store of tinned goods. Eggs were plentiful, but as villagers saved up six months' supply to present to the District Officer on his rounds they were also unreliable. Cary could, however, boast of having two houses. One, at Bussa, comprised two dilapidated rondavels open on all sides to the curiosity of hyenas and joined by a thatched roof full of holes; Cary was washed out of it altogether by the violent storms which brought the wet season of 1917 to a close. The house at Kaiama, which had stood empty for some years, was not in much better shape. 'It was falling into ruin, and in one of my two upper rooms most of the floor was hole. But this too was an advantage. I could see from my bath right down into the office and know at once what I was in for that morning: a visit from old chiefs, anxious to get up a war on the French frontier, hunters quarrelling about the correct division of a deer, one of my road gangs complaining of evil spirits who turned the edge of their tools, or a witch murder with about twenty-five witnesses, all convinced of the existence of witches and the expediency of killing them' ('Christmas in Africa').

Cary did not stay in either of these houses for more than a few

weeks at a time. He had seven districts to tour, with a view ultimately to producing a full report on the geology, flora, fauna,
population, history, crops, local industries and trade of each district.
There were no roads other than narrow bush-tracks, and no ferries
or bridges across the rivers, which were in full flood at the time of
Cary's arrival. Everything of value – clothes, food, ammunition,
Government money, even Cary's current manuscript – had to be
floated across on calabashes, eight-foot gourds grown near the river
for the purpose. Cary had enjoyed trekking in Bauchi which was a
well-developed province, but he came to dread it during his first
months in Borgu: 'I believe I have a filthy trek tomorrow with
three rivers to cross, and no canoes, which means getting soaked to
the neck, and the Emir insists on coming with me so I will have a
lot of fools prancing round me on half broke horses all the way,
and the drums and trumpets going for five hours' (26 June 1917).

Difficulties like these had been Cary's lot all through the
Cameroons campaign. What made them almost intolerable when he
first went to Borgu was loneliness. A few weeks after his arrival he
wrote to his wife: 'I was reduced to making faces at myself in my
lampshade tonight, which acts as a distorting mirror, for a little
human companionship and amusement' (13 July 1917). Five toads
which moved into his Bussa house (the mother toad, he wrote, had
quite lost her figure and looked like a pat of butter dropped from a
fourth-floor window) were welcome company: 'I understand how
people in the Bastille made friends of mice and rats and toads'
(29 August and 11 September 1917). He was fully aware that the
gravest danger of such loneliness was a loss of mental balance;
and a tart comment on H. G. Wells in a letter – 'He appears to have

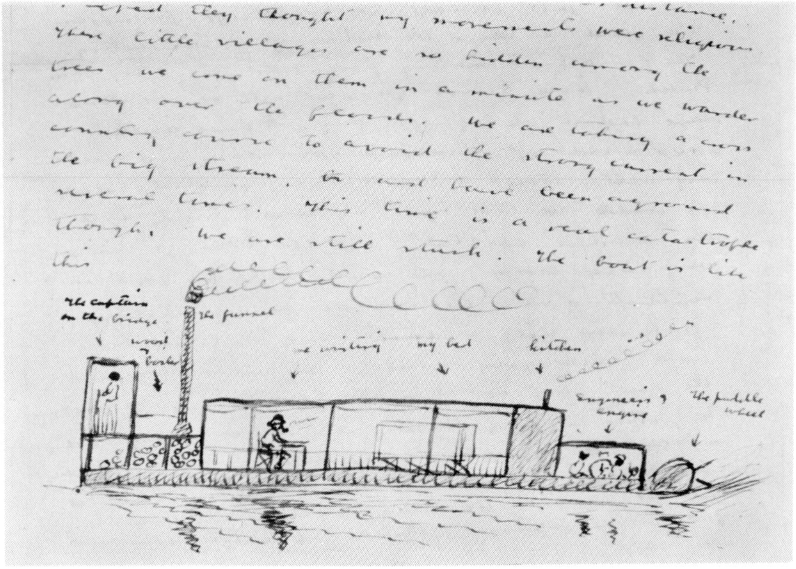

... they thought my movements were religious ... distance.
These little villages are so hidden among the
trees we come on them in a minute as we wander
along over the floods. We are taking a cross
country course to avoid the strong current in
the big stream. We must have been aground
several times. This time is a real catastrophe
though. We are still stuck. The boat is like
this

Plate I

From a letter from Joyce Cary to his wife, 22 September 1916

for myself. My office is now in pretty good order, by which I do not mean what a woman means by good order, not office. I mean that I can find any documents I want at once - that I can follow a correspondence immediately - that my various books are up to date and clearly understandable - that I can lay my hand on information, or papers or books or blotting paper in a moment. But I do not mean that there are neat piles of paper laid in useful rows in a dusted room. My books, papers etc are all stained with rain, and spotted with mud (except my private books which have a dry place) and the room is my bed-room - which is like this. You see the tent hung up over the bed, and the office in the old native bed - standing on its head against the wall.

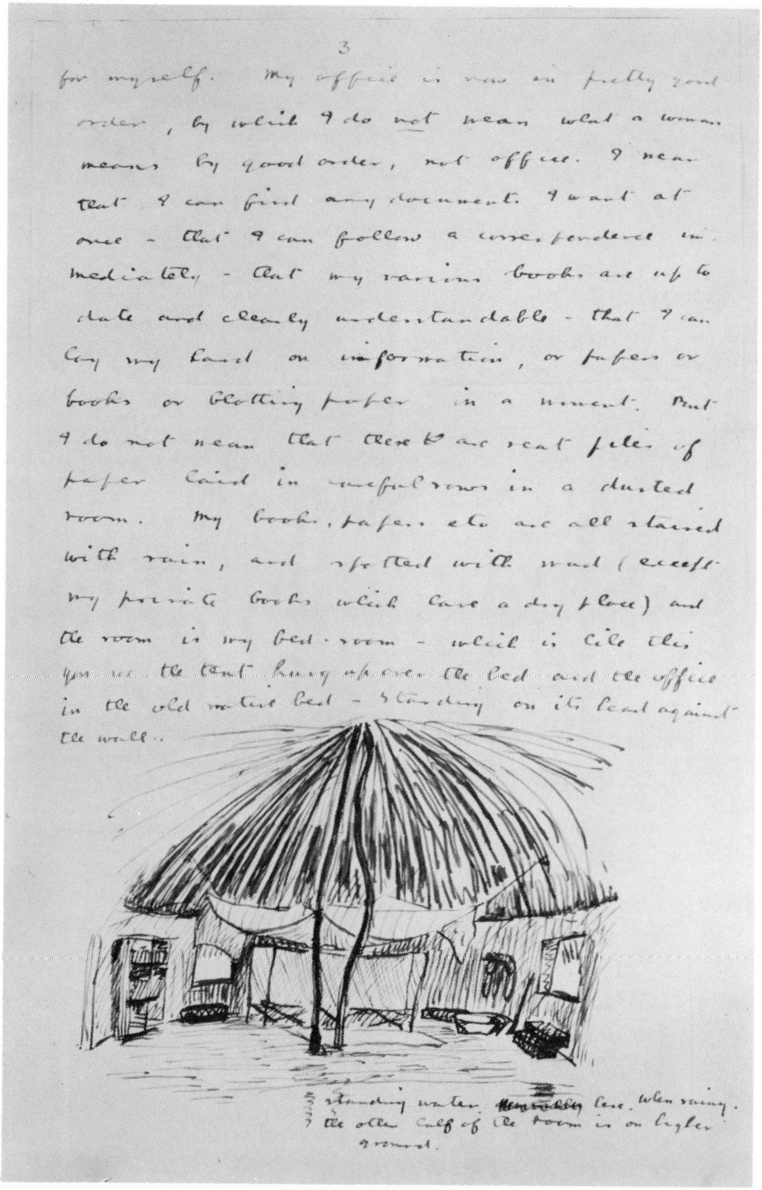

standing water. ...... less when raining. the other half of the room is on higher ground.

Plate II

From a letter from Joyce Cary to his wife, 17 October 1917

ceased to patronize the King for a moment, in order to give God a
pat on the head' – is followed by the misgiving, 'But perhaps this
is a bush-hate, a bush-hate is one of those unreasoning fancies which
seize you when you are alone in the bush. Everyone knows 'em out
here. They lead sometimes to strange and even tragic results'
(6 July 1917). In these circumstances, Cary's hunger for company
was appeased by the simplest means, and the spontaneous friendliness of small children could make his day:

> One girl was dressed in her best necklace, the other in her Sunday earring,
> and the little boy wore a bangle. They were police-children, who had
> come to salute me. This was their own idea. The smallest girl who was not
> more than 3 lost her nerve when it came to the point, burst into tears
> and fled for her life. The other two behaved with great propriety. I gave
> them pennies, and the young lady suggested that her sister ought to have
> a penny too, so I sent the sister a penny. . . . To tell the truth, I was as
> pleased as punch with this compliment and have been smiling all day. I
> could not even be severe enough in a private interview with the Emir this
> evening, who has 15 wives already, and yet insists on trying to grab other
> people's.
>
> (28 August 1917)

Cary's isolation was made the more complete by the lack of
communications. 'Do you realize', he wrote to his wife in September,
'the conditions of mails and everything else in Borgu – that I
am 80 miles from even a bush post office, when I am at Bussa, and
in July that my letters travelled over 200 miles before they reached
a post office at all – over rivers that had to be swum, and along roads
which can't be travelled except in couples – carried too by pagans
who have no conception of time or urgency – or what a mail
means' (3 September 1917). There was no telegraph, and Cary had
to wait a week to ten days for an answer to a letter to the Provincial
Office. Before he had left Kontagora he had been told that on
account of this lack of communications he would have to act for
himself in any crisis and rely on the Resident to back him up.

This perhaps was the worst aspect of his isolation: Cary was
solely responsible for the good government of people whose ways
of life and processes of thought were impenetrably strange to him.

He had had practically no political experience; as he admitted in one of his letters, nearly all his time in Nigeria had been spent soldiering or arranging for the transport of troops. Ever since his return to the country he had lived the insulated life of a European station, in Africa but not of it, which he later satirized in *The African Witch*. Now he had to deal unaided with such problems as the mysterious disappearance of an entire village. A spirit had come and played a drum all night in the top·of a tree. 'This was too much for the villagers, and they ran. But one does not laugh so easily at these things when one has spent some time in the middle of Africa. There is no place where the night is so full of strange noises, or where trees, hills clouds and rocks take stranger shapes. . . . I think I should try a scattergun on this ghost, but it is risky here to interfere with superstitions. You never know what you are up against, natural phenomena, a madman, a swindler, or a powerful secret organization' (17 July 1917).

The difficulty about any kind of enquiry into this or other, graver problems, was that Cary found he was not told the truth, but whatever was thought to appease or gratify him. Thirty years later he was able to see that this was the inevitable result of his being a kind of bush dictator; no dictator is told the truth, because no one knows what use he will make of it. But in 1917 Cary was still too inexperienced in government and too apprehensive of unrest in the division to see the problem with this kind of detachment. There had already been serious trouble in Borgu because the easy-going District Officer at Yelwa had allowed himself to be hoodwinked by the Emir of Bussa and his courtiers. Dread of the same thing happening again made Cary complain about the lies (all wrapped in elaborate compliments) which he was told morning after morning as he sat in his office hearing disputes, trying cases or weighing up the totally contradictory reports of the Waziri (Vizier) and the Political Agent, each of whom hinted that the other was lying for his own advantage. The haunting anxieties·of this time were still vivid to Cary in 1951, when he wrote in an American periodical: 'No one, not placed in such a situation, can fully realize the sense of blindness and distrust which took possession of me in those first months of solitude in Borgu. I say took possession – because it was at once like a foreign invader seizing on my mind, and a kind of demon. I would wake up at night and feel as if the dark itself were an immense black brain, meditating, behind its thick featureless countenance, some deep plan for a new and still more surprising outbreak' ('Africa Yester-day'). And another article of the fifties sums up the dejection Cary experienced on his arrival in Borgu: 'At my first coming I had hated it. I had left an Emirate of the North with its desert traders, its pageant of horsemen, and got in return this twelve thousand miles of waste' ('Christmas in Africa').

4

It was not surprising that in July of 1917 Cary's wife wrote urging him to leave the Nigerian service. He replied shortly that this was not possible; he could not throw up a certain salary and a pension for a writer's uncertain income. Besides this he had to admit, by the middle of August, that his view of Borgu was changing rapidly. He even asserts that 'these three months have been some of the happiest I have spent.' Although this was a major overstatement, meant to allay his wife's anxiety, another letter written during an evening storm in late September shows that he had by then adjusted himself in a remarkable way to his new life:

I always feel more lonely d'you know in a thunderstorm, when the rain begins to fall. The splash, splash all round the eaves into the full drains and I might add the splash splash through the roof into full pools in the house have a very dreary sound. I've been four months alone now – considerably longer than I was married, but I haven't been unhappy. I've done really a good deal of work of all sorts official and otherwise, and I've found out a good deal about myself. One does in solitude. I often wondered how I should stand being alone. . . . I haven't exchanged a word of rational conversation since May, and this is getting on to the end of September. When I do talk English, I have to pick up the simplest words and repeat my meaning in two or three forms. . . . All this makes it easy for me to understand the queer cases out here of fellows drinking themselves to death, getting homicidal mania, or breaking down nervously into neurotic wrecks, when in the back bush by themselves – though I myself am as fit as a flea, and suffer no ill effects at all. Partly this is because I know what to guard against – nerves – drink – idleness etc. – and partly because I have always been able to extract a very high degree of pleasure out of books, and almost companionship.

(22 September 1917)

What Cary later described as the 'intense mental life' he led in Borgu was nourished first and foremost by the contents of his book-case in the mud house at Bussa: predominantly novels by Cervantes, Balzac, Thackeray, Hardy, and Conrad. He read each of them three or four times and discussed them in detail in his letters. One comment on his reading is illuminating for the insight it affords into the way that Cary, once he was thrown entirely on his own resources, began to shed the social prejudices of his earlier days in the colonial service: 'I ask myself now why do I object to that – is it really bad, or is it because I'm prejudiced by something that's nothing to do with the book at all. Do I dislike that, because I'm a varsity man, or a government official, or married, or bald, or blind, or for anything I've been taught to believe, which is really affectation or prudery or snobbery, or prejudice, and which I have allowed to stick in my brain unnoticed till its dangerous like a fungus, and is beginning to make my brains all mouldy' (10 September 1917).

Together with his reading, Cary's writing kept him (he told his wife) from 'going mad or becoming a vegetable' in Borgu. He had begun to write again very soon after his arrival in the division, and was 'happy every hour of the day in consequence', though he found it difficult to finish anything. A story called 'The Episode', which promised to develop into a novel was described, when he abandoned it a month later, as 'the twentieth this tour'. In actual bulk, Cary wrote the equivalent of three novels during this tour of duty. Nothing of this has survived, as at the first news that he was to be relieved by the end of the year he burnt the lot.

While reading and writing made Cary's lonely leisure hours

something more than tolerable, his anxieties over his official position were subsiding as he grew more used to political work. Cary's motives in going to Nigeria had included a good measure of idealism: he wanted to give the people in his care peace and justice. But now that forty thousand people were actually in his care, he found that corruption made it wellnigh impossible for him to fulfil this ideal. This discovery was one reason for the unhappiness of his first few weeks in the division. 'You can't get rid of corruption in these parts; you can only stop it going on the bust', was the advice of the political officer who had tried to eradicate the worst abuses just before Cary's arrival. Cary in his turn learnt, like Bradgate in *Aissa Saved*, to have 'ears and eyes all round him: blind eyes and deaf ears'. Facts had, however, to be known before the decision whether or not to turn a blind eye to them could be made. The problem was how to get the facts. Edwardes, whose route to a new post in Sokoto brought him into chance contact with Cary on his way to Borgu, had a helpful suggestion. This was that Cary should make it his practice when on tour to sleep at some distance from the rest of his camp. Cary took this advice and after some weeks the stratagem worked: urgent voices began to whisper out of the darkness, voices full of bitterness. Sometimes the cause of the bitterness was trivial; but sometimes the complaints were indicative of quite serious injustice. The more conventional Cary of his Nafada days would have been outraged by this method of keeping in touch with what was going on in the division. Cary in Borgu was discovering, however, that 'a man in real responsibility for other people's lives and happiness had no scruples about dignity' ('Africa Yesterday'). He also knew by now that this custom afforded people literally the only free access they had to him. Anyone attempting to approach him through messengers or orderly was likely to have to pay for the privilege.

After a couple of months alone, Cary began to feel that he knew a reasonable amount about Borgu politics and was philosophically resigned to the fact that there was a great deal he never would know: 'Of course there are a 1000 cheateries going on I know nothing about, I dare say I shall still be defrauded of hundreds of cows – but things promise better. I have no illusions about my own actual wisdom. I know the old rascals in the market place could tell me a thing or two' (25 July 1917). Moreover, he was finding, to his great pleasure, that the responsibilities of a bush officer need not be a burden and could in fact be an opportunity. 'I saw how lucky I was in an exile that made me my own master. Just because Borgu was remote and cut off, just because I had no wire, I had been given free leave to make quick decisions, in fact to do what I liked. And there was always interesting and practical work in hand, mapping, road-making, bridge-building, the founding of markets and towns, the training of native staff; work I preferred very much to the end-less minute writing and form filling of a big station in a rich pro-vince' ('Christmas in Africa'). Cary in fact accomplished a great deal in the seven months of his first tour. He doubled the receipts from cattle tax, started ferries and markets and inaugurated one of the earliest adult education classes in Nigeria. This was a group of *mallams*, or Moslems literate in Arabic, whom Cary wanted taught the Roman ABC and a little arithmetic so that they could help in a census. He put them under the tuition of the Assistant Treasurer, a youth just back from the school for chiefs' sons at Kaduna. The *mallams* were all greybeards, but they were eager pupils: 'a learned man out here is always anxious for new learning, contrary to the European plan'. Court cases, mostly matrimonial disputes, were going much better than Cary, aware of his ignorance of local customs, had dared to hope they would. Before long he was con-gratulating himself on 'knowing how to manage the black man'.

The phrase is ominous; it shows that Cary had not yet really outgrown the '*laager* mentality' which prevailed among Europeans in Africa at the period, although no traces of it were to be found among the devoted pagan men whom he had admired in Bauchi. In his handling of witchcraft cases, which were frequent, Cary showed much tolerance of the incomprehensible, but little readiness to comprehend. 'I can't of course tell them their religion is worse than nonsense' is a typical comment. And sometimes in his letters his patience broke down and he indulged in a Rackham-like diatribe against the whole Negro race.

For Cary at the end of 1917, just before his leave, was still isolated, though he had learnt to enjoy his isolation. He had discovered new sources of strength in himself and in his pride in his work; but not any new interests in the country. The popularly-written article 'Christmas in Africa' captures this contentment in isolation in its account of how Cary listened from the upper verandah of his Kaiama house to the Christmas drumming in the village down the hill. Cary speaks here of the bond between himself and the drummers; but the only sympathy he in fact felt with the Borgawa, a thousand years apart from him in time, was their common defiance of nature's inhumanity of which the drums seemed to speak. 'Another advantage of my tall house on its hill was that it gave me command from my balcony of a long stretch of that same desolate Borgu bush whose emptiness, whose mean little, twisted trees, disturbed by yearly fires, spread for everlasting over its stony hills, had once so disgusted me. For that very desolation, the want of all romantic airs, had now become its charm. . . . And looking now outwards, over the bush stretching in the bright steel starlight up to the sky, a lazy ocean of blue black waves, I felt again that savage indifference which was at once its attraction and its estrangement' (MS. version).

Borgu
1918 – 1919

I

In the early months of 1918, Jarimi, a native of a village near Kaiama, contracted leprosy. Two of his three wives were taken from him by their families. He told the third wife that she might get a child by another man; but he added the warning: 'The child is mine and if you take him out of the house after I die, I will come back and kill you.' When the wife became pregnant, the village priest came to Jarimi and said, 'The baby your wife is going to bear is a juju baby and will belong to me.' Jarimi declared, 'This baby will be the death of us both'; and in fulfilment of this he took his bow and shot the priest, who died begging the bystanders to see that his debt of three shillings to the village chief was paid.

Joyce Cary heard of the murder early in October, on his journey back from leave. 'I hear they have caught a murderer at Kaiama. Rather a nuisance if I have to hang a man. I shouldn't like that at all. I haven't a notion how it is done, and I don't know how I should feel either. It is rather hard to have to try a man and hang him too. I would much rather have him shot. However, perhaps I'll acquit him. Or perhaps Hammy [Hamilton-Browne, the Resident] will try him' (8 October 1918).

The procedure in a case like this was for Cary, after the preliminary inquiry, to inform his Resident that a case had arisen which needed to be tried in the Provincial Court; and for the Resident then to decide whether he wanted to undertake it himself or to apply for a commission giving full juridical powers to the officer on the spot. The delay involved was not without value. Once while

Cary was waiting for instructions about three self-confessed murderers, their supposed victims turned up alive and well. The three
men, having made medicine against their enemies, had taken the
wish for the deed. In the case of Rex *v.* Jarimi the Resident at Kontagora asked for a commission on the grounds that it would be best if
the witnesses could be sworn on their local sacred object; Cary
received the commission on his return from an assessment tour of
the immediate district, and tried the case early in December.

At the trial, Jarimi's attitude was one of fatalistic despair – 'I
don't want to have anything more to do with anyone' – and the
best Cary could do for him was to make a strong recommendation
to mercy 'on account of the provocation'. The trial, which came at a
time when Cary was anxious about his wife's second confinement
and when he was suffering from the 1918 influenza, left him feeling
wretchedly depressed. Fortunately, his recommendation to mercy
was accepted, so he never found himself in the quandary of Rudbeck
in *Mister Johnson*, although the letter I have quoted shows that he
had already envisaged Rudbeck's solution.

This episode is typical of Cary's much deeper involvement, in
this second tour in Borgu, with the people of the division. He was
no longer 'a man in a tower', cut off from the Borgawa. For one
thing he spent a great deal of the fifteen-month tour in moving
about the division on tax assessment work. He planned to cover four
of his seven districts, although in the end interruptions prevented
his assessing more than two. But the interruptions themselves kept
him on the move: one was a boundary commission which took him
to the extreme Agwarra end of the division, and the other a fantastic
episode in which Cary was told to close the office and abandon the
division altogether. He had to take a procession of a hundred and
thirty-five people – servants, staff, police, prisoners, and bearers
carrying all his possessions and the office equipment – as far as
Kontagora, where he was informed that the division was not to be
closed after all and that he could march them all back to Kaiama to
resume work.

All this touring gave Cary the chance of map-making, which he loved. The existing maps of Borgu were worse than useless. Lugard, in describing his Borgu expedition, had warned travellers against accepting descriptive names as proper ones; in fact, against compiling maps which, like Cock Jarvis's in *Castle Corner*, bore names like 'Town Town, River River, Idontknow Village, Begyourpardon Rock.' Such names serve to remind us that even map-making was a social activity, not solely dependent on the right use of a prismatic compass. Cary in fact got some enthusiastic local co-operation in his map-making from Lafia, the new court scribe and another product of the school for chiefs' sons, whom he sent off with a kitchen clock to time his coverage of thirty-eight miles. Cary omitted to tell him to stop for the night, and he walked the whole distance in a day. Although his feat was not quite as astonishing as Cary made it sound in the Carfax preface to *Aissa Saved*, it earned Lafia the distinction of being the book's original hero.

Mapping, however, was only incidental to Cary's main task of making a field study of each district in order to assess its taxability. The usual method of lump-sum assessment did not appeal to him, as a passage in *The African Witch* indicates. The book's hero, Aladai, has to do sums 'for anxious chiefs required by government to divide a total tax of thirty-two pounds seven shillings and fourpence equitably between nine families, all differing in size and wealth: two butchers with farms; one dyer with a horse but no farm; the village idiot; a widow with two grown-up sons, one a prosperous thief; and a fisherman suspected of being, at will, a hyena, and possessing unknown sources of income' (pp. 105-6). The only alternative to this, setting aside a straight capitation tax, was individual assessment, and this Cary undertook almost single-handed. His only help was from his *mallams* who, previous to the assessment, went through the district taking the name of each member of each family. When Cary arrived in a village his table and chair would be set up under a tree and all the families assembled. They were amused and impressed when Cary, whom most of them had never seen before, read out their names from his big book, into which Lafia had transcribed the *mallams'* lists.

As Lugard repeatedly said, the merit of such careful assessment was that it brought the administrator into close contact with the people. Cary agreed with him:

I have been through three small villages today, and seen every creature, and talked with most. I think with the Governor that assessment work is valuable 'not only in its express purpose of adjusting tax, but also in making an officer acquainted with his Division'. I have made more acquaintances today than for a long time past, and with a great deal of pleasure. I find lonely men in lonely huts working hard all the year to support one old blind father, and a child — or chiefs in old age still cheerful and undaunted with nobody left in their tumbledown hamlet but a leper or so, and one household. . . . They respect and care for the old, they feed the sick and the poor — there are no cases here of people starved to death — they pet and spoil their children. What would be wrong with us, is wrong with them. It is true that many things which are wrong to us are not wrong to them, but it is a question whether they are essentials.

(9 November 1918)

Although Cary was later to say that his long and elaborate notes on native customs were 'completely useless from a scientific point of view', they earned him gubernatorial praise for 'the very close scrutiny which has been brought to bear upon local conditions'. More important than this, they compelled him to think himself, for the first time, into the minds and situations of a primitive people. True, he was at the time himself too strong a rebel against organized religion to be able to show in his reports much tolerance of the practices of Borgawa priests, who are always dismissed as 'juju men'. But he tried hard to divest himself of prejudice when he discussed the attitudes of the Borgawa to birth and death. One belief that was rife in Borgu, as it still is everywhere in Nigeria and is likely to remain so while infant mortality is high, was that children could be reborn to their parents. Cary's struggle to see this from the Borgawa point of view can be felt in this extract from his assessment report on the Yashikera district:

A child who dies is said to return. A wife, whose children always die, will make a mark on the body of a baby, to see if it is the same baby who continues to play this spiteful trick upon her. There are several children now living in Yashikera who are said to have been marked thus, on their first or second death, or return, to have shown the mark when reborn, and to survive with it now. Such a baby, the fourth or fifth of a family who have all died, will be received with abuse and given a contemptuous name. It is often sold, to humiliate it. The mother puts it in a calabash and accosts some friend with 'Will you buy this?' The friend offers ten pounds, which is accepted, and pays a few anini, which are generally strung round the baby's neck. The naming of the ten pounds is to deceive the baby. Such a baby will be named Bawa. The buyer has, of course, no rights over his purchase, but if the baby grows up, he is expected to treat this financial godfather as a benefactor. He will be called Master, and welcomed in the house of the child's parents.

The abuse, the sale, the scornful name have all one object, to make the baby think it is not wanted. Its evil spirit which has already played so many tricks on its mother, will then, it is fairly expected, try to play another, by staying alive.

The point of view should be noticed – the parents believe that the child dies to spite them. Pity for the baby is by no means the first thought, as might be usual among Europeans. But I do not urge this as a proof of callousness, because it is obvious that the whole native argument hangs upon the ability of the child to cause his parents suffering by dying. In Borgu as elsewhere the people are devoted to children.

Nevertheless, there is a difference in the sorrow, which is worth remarking as a racial difference. The European, I think, is sorry not only for his own loss, but for the baby's failure to live and use his life, perhaps is sorrier on the baby's account than his own, while the native, in Yashikera at least, feels pain at his own misfortune, and has no sympathy at all for the child. But then again, as has been seen, he believes that the child can be born again if it chooses, so that it is logical for him to see himself as the injured person.

Careful reflection such as this on the differences between group values enabled Cary to judge cases involving Borgawa beliefs with admirable fairness. If his immediate reaction to the news that three people in Kaiama had been accused of killing a baby because it was a witch was 'I shall hang the man if I can', the record of the actual trial shows how objective he was able to be in the end. The child had fallen on its face at birth, a sure sign it was a witch, and the occupants of the compound fled in terror. The grandfather, a man called Bio, then took charge of matters. He sent back a woman, who made the

mother give her quite substantial payment for removing the child:
'If you don't pay me, the baby will kill you all.' A second woman
then took the child away in a calabash. A small, thin person, looking
'like any old European woman hired to wash a floor', she had (Cary
recalled many years later) been killing such children for the last
thirty years, right under the nose of a succession of district officers.
No one betrayed her 'for the good reason that all natives feared to
betray one so brave, powerful and useful to the community' (N85).
She was calm and resigned at the trial, because she realized that it
was the revengeful spirit of the witch children who had delivered
her into Cary's hands. This in itself made the judgement difficult,
since Cary had to avoid strengthening a local belief in the sinister
ability of witches to co-operate with the Government. So the two
women got off lightly. In judging Bio, Cary had to weigh up the
very real fear of a witch child in the district against the fact that a
more enlightened attitude was growing up; the local chief had tried
hard to dissuade Bio from making away with the baby. Bio was
found guilty and condemned, but with a strong plea for mercy 'and
a comparatively short sentence on account of the local circumstances
affecting his moral responsibility'. This plea was allowed. Perhaps
the legal advisers at Kaduna realized the possibility, which seems to
have escaped Cary at the time, that a child left untended for some
hours after birth would have been dead by the time it was taken
away. The case and others like it bring sharply before a modern
reader the appalling responsibility laid upon young administrators
under Lugard's system; they had to combine the functions of judge
and jury, clerk of the court and counsel for the defence in cases of
the utmost gravity, involving people whose code of behaviour was
fundamentally different from their own.

Cary tried one other witchcraft case in the Provincial Court. An
attractive young wife had been accused of witchcraft by her sisters-
in-law. Their husbands beat the girl and tied her up. In her terror
she promised to reveal the name of the real witch, but could not
even manage to invent one. She then escaped, but, having her arms
tied, either died of hunger in the bush or was killed by animals; and

the discovery of her half-eaten body led to four of the family concerned being charged with manslaughter. Once again Cary ap-
pealed for leniency: 'It should be remembered that the prisoners,
tho' guilty of a cruel injustice, did not intend the result, that this is
the first prosecution of the kind in the neighbourhood, and a long
sentence to these bush pagans, involving transfer to a central gaol,
would certainly be a sentence of death, as they would pine away'
(Borgu Court minute-book, p. 28).

In cases like these as in innumerable less serious ones Cary seems
to have felt, over and above a wish to understand native customs
and beliefs, an almost Conradian sense of community with the man
who put himself on the wrong side of the law. It shows itself in his
letters when he expresses concern over 'a noted rebel' hiding in the
perilous bush – 'I'm sorry for the man who has been very unjustly
treated' – or over an escaped prisoner who might try to swim a
crocodile-infested river – 'I am worried that the poor man should
be eaten, when his sentence is only a year and he would have been
home again against next harvest.' At other times Cary expresses the
instinctive sympathy which he was to show throughout his novels
for the man who could carry off his misfortunes with *panache*:

> I sent a mallam off to prison today. And when I ordered them to take him
> away—he came up and salaamed. It was not in mockery—but pride.
> There is a greatness in these fellows—Mohomedans. They have all the
> grand bearing and tradition of the French noblesse in the Terror. Though
> he is a rascal—he is a gentleman—and I find rascality loses much of its
> bad appearance when joined to a high manner, perfect self-possession,
> and great courage. The man did not move an eyelid. And I noticed he
> wore his best clothes. Yet he is ruined, and he has been accustomed to be
> a big man, with great power. He ought not to have had the power, but
> he obtained it – that was his undoing.
>
> (5 May 1919)

The indirections and flattery which were a normal part of Moslem
social intercourse could, however, be exasperating. Cases in court
took three times as long as was necessary while appellant and
defendant salaamed and showed themselves, in Cary's phrase, great
ones for the butter-shovel:

They madden me sometimes when I am very busy, and have a dozen [cases] waiting to be heard – by starting like this 'I never tell a lie. I would not dare to tell a lie to the white man, the powerful one. I know it is no good (What's your name? from me) God prolong your life, O King, lord of Justice (What's your name and what do you want?) I thank God that you are ruler of the land' – and so on. The compliments take ten minutes – the business two. A morning of petty cases is bad for the temper. Especially as the most complimentary tell the biggest lies. The simple country pagan, who stares at one with a stony gaze, and bursts into his grievance without any circumlocution whatever (tho' he generally begins at the end) is a far more pleasant subject. He starts simply. 'She hit me on the head and says she doesn't want me any more. She took her home, and she says she won't let her come back, because *she* is always cursing her.' And by a little questioning it is not difficult to find out how many different shes are involved, and what is their relationship. It is generally the first wife, the second wife, and a mother-in-law.

(30 August 1919)

The patience and tolerance which were required of a political officer working under the system of indirect rule, even in a division where the Emirs had such restricted powers as they had in Borgu, are shown in Cary's handling of one case of corruption which printed itself on his memory. The Emir of Kaiama – a gentle old man, rather like the Emir in *Aissa Saved*, according to Cary himself – agreed with Cary over the teacups that the chief in question, who was despotic and stupid, should be publicly tried and, if found guilty, deposed. The Resident acquiesced. The trial was a full-dress affair, with Cary seated on the best office chair by the side of the Emir. The chief not only confessed to extortion but to quite a few other crimes that Cary had not known about. Cary gave his judgement that the Sarkin was unfitted to be a chief, and asked the Emir for his opinion. The Emir, who had received a number of confidential visits between the tea-party and the trial, promptly said he thought the Sarkin ought to be given another chance. 'The whole assembly looked at me', Cary wrote later. 'I felt like a fool and probably looked like a fool. But I was obliged to say "In that case O will remain chief"' (N85).

Cary's growing understanding of Borgawa customs and values shows itself in many other ways in his letters of 1918 and 1919. For instance, he no longer cursed the royal entries arranged for him by the Emirs. Instead, he felt sorry for the aching arms of the umbrella man – 'but it would be rude to refuse'. Cary in fact showed signs during this tour of becoming not only paternalistic towards the people of his division, but also jealously protective of their way of life. The news that a missionary had appeared in Kaiama while Cary was on tour, only to vanish in a pointed manner before his return, produced a diatribe against the Machiavellian ways of missionaries. Cary complained, as Bewsher of *An American Visitor* might have done, that the missionaries, in their eagerness to turn pagans into the 'hybrids we see in the coast towns' completely misjudged the policy of indirect rule. There was in fact some cause for Cary's anxiety. The sect in question was so bigoted that, in his own words, 'the Wee Frees are Catholic to them'. Cary feared for the peace of the division if ultra-Protestant enthusiasm was kindled among the Borgawa: 'I have no intention of getting scuppered in a religious war' (24 April 1919). The kind of trouble he could foresee remained fresh in his imagination for ten years, to furnish some of the liveliest incidents of *Aissa Saved*.

It was, however, rare for Cary's increasing concern for the people of his division to take this negatively protective form. As Cary's knowledge of the Borgawa deepened, he felt more and more the wish to free them from their poverty and limited horizons by developing the division on the lines he had envisaged during his first tour:

> I walked out this evening two miles up the road – by myself. And the women I passed went down on one knee, and the men bowed their heads literally to the dust, and cried out, 'Lord', even farmers a quarter of a mile away in the fields hailed me, and salaamed, and I thought how strange it would look to our democratic Europe – and what a little person I am in reality. Who knows me at home – but 25,000 people here call me 'Baba' or Father. Of course they call Diggle Baba too, or anyone else who is sent. And they don't care twopence for me really – there's no

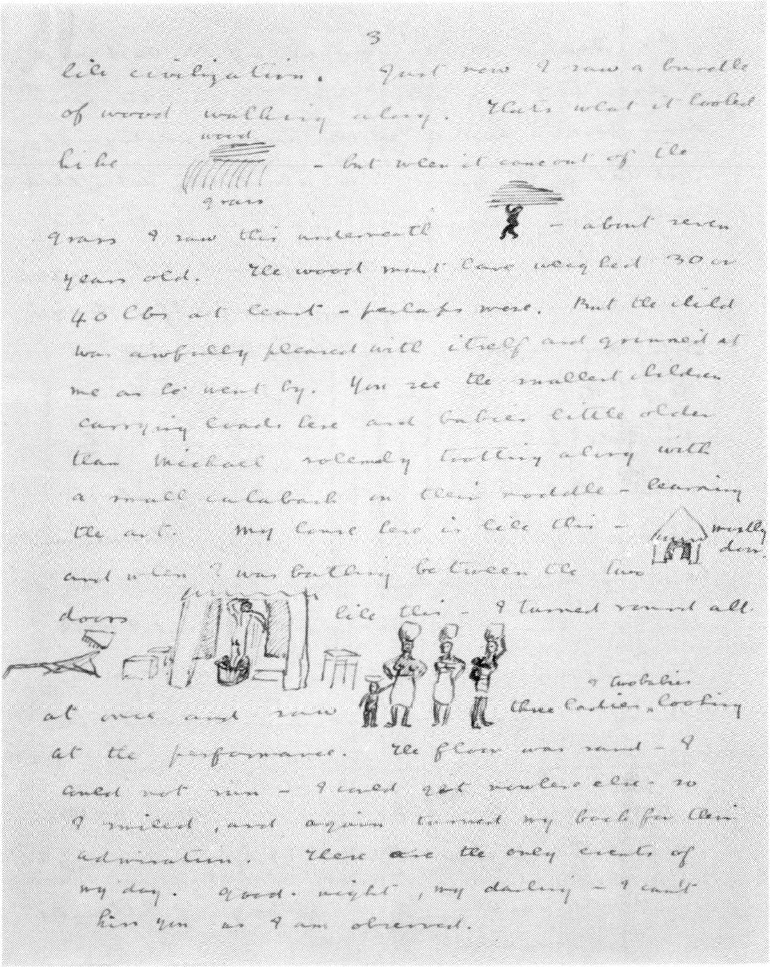

3

like civilization. Just now I saw a bundle of wood walking along. That's what it looked like [wood / grass] — but when it came out of the grass I saw this underneath [figure] — about seven years old. The wood must have weighed 30 or 40 lbs at least — perhaps more. But the child was awfully pleased with itself and grinned at me as he went by. You see the smallest children carrying loads here and babies little older than Michael solemnly trotting along with a small calabash on their noddle — learning the art. My close here is like this — [sketch] mostly down and when I was bathing between the two doors [sketch] like this — I turned round all at once and saw three ladies looking 2 babies at the performance. The floor was sand — I could not run — I could get nowhere else — so I smiled, and again turned my back for their admiration. These are the only events of my day. Good-night, my darling — I can't kiss you as I am observed.

Plate III

From a letter from Joyce Cary to his wife, 10 February 1919

goodness knows I work at it – but I accomplish very very little. However I shall probably be quite cheerful again next week.

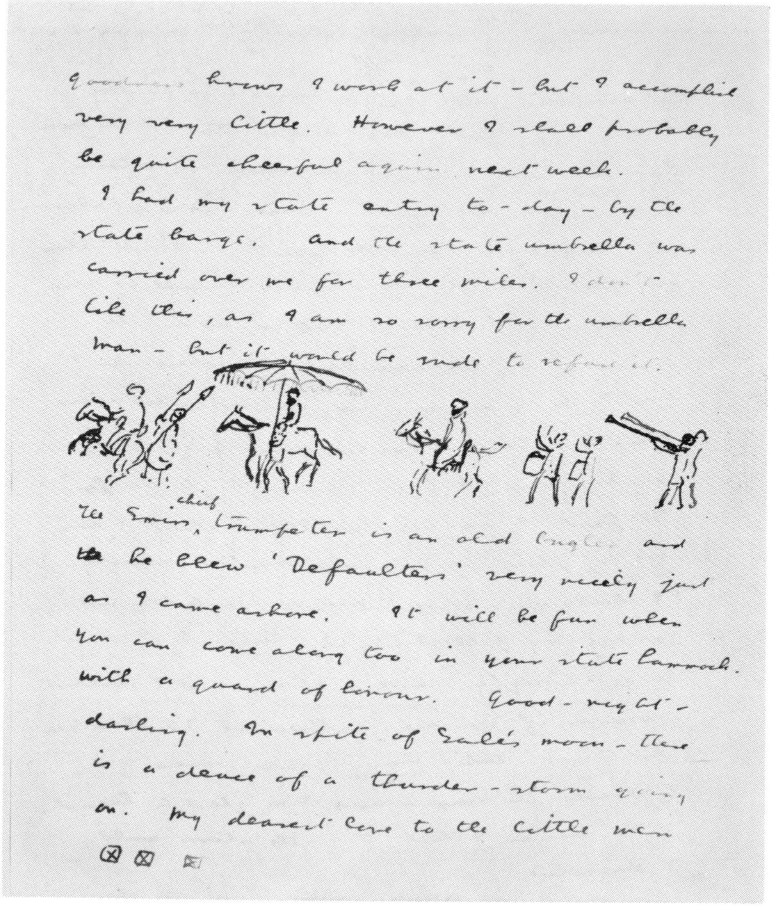

I had my state entry to-day – by the state barge. And the state umbrella was carried over me for three miles. I don't like this, as I am so sorry for the umbrella man – but it would be rude to refuse it.

The Smin, chief trumpeter is an old bugler and he blew 'Defaulters' very nicely just as I came ashore. It will be fun when you can come along too in your state barouche with a guard of honour. Good-night darling. In spite of Sale's moon – there is a deuce of a thunder-storm going on. My dearest love to the little men

Plate IV

From a letter from Joyce Cary to his wife, 12 April 1919. The reference in the first two lines is to his writing

affection, or loyalty – only respect. I think more of them than they think of me – like the Tsar and his people. Yet they run to me when they are in trouble, and they depend on me for much – for protection from tyranny, and exploitation, and injustice. I could do more for them if I was allowed to spend a little more money – I want a vaccinator and a vet – I want an engineer and some bigger bridges than can be made with bush-timber – I want some better roads – and a larger staff.

(29 May 1919)

2

Bridge-building absorbed a great part of Cary's energies in the dry season of 1918 to 1919. Even without an engineer and with only local bush timber, he was able to build twelve large bridges during the tour, one of them seventy yards long and twenty-five feet wide:

> I really did enjoy myself today. When I went out four miles at six, and found 200 people waiting and piles of timber, and palm planks, I felt some nervousness. For my bridge was only a dream bridge. I've never built one before – and the truth is I only had a vague design in my head – no drawings made – in rather a haphazard way. The bridge had to be about 16 feet high and the fresh cut timbers were hard to handle with no ropes. I looked bold however – marched about very confidently – stuck in my heel and said 'dig here' (the bed is dry now of course) and got up the first huge gofa successfully. A gofa is a forked stick. The ones on each side however had to lean in. And I had a bad moment when the first began to lean too far. Just in time we got it propped. And then suddenly things began to move, and in about 20 minutes my first trestle was up. . . . I have a grudge against this river as it has given me many wettings, and one panic, when I thought I was going to be a demnition corpse as Mr. Mantalini would say.

(27 February 1919)

The bridges he built in Borgu gave Cary more satisfaction than anything else he did there. They saved lives; and traders deviated fifty miles from their ordinary route in order to make sure of a dry crossing. There were of course many setbacks to the bridge building, which are recorded, almost exactly as they occurred, in *Aissa Saved*. One serious difficulty was that sketch-plans were meaningless to people who had never seen a drawing and could therefore not translate something two-dimensional into solid fact. But Cary found that his bridge building, like his mapping, brought the man of imagination out of the crowd. The man of imagination in this case was called Tasuki. He is described in *The Case for African Freedom* as small, ragged and dirty, full of disease and covered with bruises – 'Yet he had more brains, guts, and power of leadership than many of those Emirate officials who had taken their pay for fifteen years to neglect the Borgu roads and leave the streams un-bridged' (p. 124). Tasuki, faced with the problem of getting whole tree trunks into a vertical position, improvised a multiple pulley with tie-tie, or liana, and a double-forked tree. He had never heard of such a device; he simply thought it out for himself.

In all his enterprises at this time Cary was struck by the difference between the apathetic many, who could not connect one idea with another sufficiently to be able to envisage what they had not already seen, and the rare man or woman gifted with an imagination that could be worked upon to make progress possible. This imagination was most often found among those with experience which went a little further than their own village. Lafia, back from the school for chiefs' sons, displayed it. So did Musa, the Political Agent. A native of Lokoja, he was urbane, cynical, rather lazy and cer-tainly not incorruptible. But Cary developed a very real regard for him during their long tours together, because he had both foresight and insight. The same qualities were displayed in the young clerk, Mr Graves, sent to the division in August of 1919. Cary's letters of the time show that at first Graves was a disappointment to him. But one day Graves surprised Cary by presenting him with a report that he had sat up all night to copy; he did not want the District Officer to get into trouble at headquarters by missing the mail. This seemed to Cary to stem from an imaginative reach which could be attained by very few of the people among whom he lived. Again, when Cary demonstrated, with the help of a sufferer from guinea-worm, how the worm laid its eggs in water, he had the mortification, the same day, of seeing people who had watched the demonstration drinking unfiltered water from the same pool. Yet even there his teaching went home to someone; a woman later sought divorce on the grounds that her husband had caught guinea-worm which he could have avoided if he had drunk clean water. Meanwhile, Cary realized, wells were the answer to the ten per cent. incidence of the parasite in Kaiama; and on one of his brief returns to the station during this tour he sank the wells from which the women of Kaiama, swathed in their bright cottons, still draw clean water.

Cary was back in Kaiama for the last few months of 1919, writing up his latest assessment report and preparing his annual returns. But this office work absorbed only a small part of his time and energy.

The return of the dry season gave him the chance for a new venture, the building of proper roads in place of the bush tracks which could be traversed only on foot or on an agile pony. Edwardes's book on native paths served as a guide. Tasuki was sent off on a surveying expedition and delighted Cary once more by his capability. 'There are two useless kinds of subordinate – those who are such fools that they do nothing right, and those who are so clever that they do everything wrong. This man comes between – a capable fellow' (23 August 1919). A month's work on the road sent Tasuki's reputation even higher: 'He is the most precious of discoveries, a man who can do a job with a conscience' (23 September 1919). Once again

Tasuki's pioneer mind distinguished him from the crowd, this time the crowd of road builders who could not understand the need for a cambered surface and whose enthusiasm flagged to a standstill when the road began to pass through uninhabited country. The solution to this last problem was to start roadside markets for the road gangs and for the travellers who were to use the road. Travellers also needed safe lodgings at night, especially if they were foreign traders from the edge of the desert. To give them security, Cary built zungos, or simple inns like the one described in *Mister Johnson*. These were a great financial success. Though each had to have a paid innkeeper, and though the charge was only a penny for a man or horse and a halfpenny for a woman or goat, the zungos had brought in a profit of a hundred and thirty pounds for the Treasury by the time Cary left Borgu.

The tone of many of Cary's Kaiama letters written in the last months of 1919 is wildly happy. His bridges had saved lives; his bridges, roads, zungos and markets had brought a steep increase in trade. He had found individuals who shared his pride in these achievements and who could extend them all over the division. He had also something they could not share, the educated man's feeling for historical processes, which gave him the knowledge he was building for a future he would not see:

> I thought as I walked along ... this is as some Roman engineer felt when he strolled down the long reaches of Watling Street, and wondered how long he would be permitted to foretell the future of Britain – with one eye on the disturbances of Rome. Shall we all be recalled by the breaking of the Empire. And shall some Blackman in the year 4,000 trace my road for a paper in the Kaiama Archaeological Society, and debate learnedly the ancient greatness of Britain. It is certain. Nothing endures for ever. England will become little England again and Nigeria an Empire of the blacks – India of the browns.

> (4 October 1919)

There is an undertone of melancholy in these speculations which is the aftermath of Cary's excitement at seeing his road take shape before his eyes. Four days later he admits, like any other artist, that he has lost interest in the road now that it is nearly finished. He was experiencing the lassitude he makes Rudbeck feel at the end of his roadmaking effort in *Mister Johnson*. And like Rudbeck, he was finding that the authorities took little interest in his achievements. His appeal for a few steel girders, some good tackle and a carpenter, to help him build more and better bridges, met with no response. His road vote was sixty pounds a year for the clearing of bush tracks. For the zungos, which were regarded in Kaduna as a fanciful bit of extravagance, he got nothing. In *The Case for African Freedom* Cary describes how the Resident scraped together a few pounds from the provincial treasury and Cary himself added his allowances for 'police uniforms, stationery, miscellaneous and secret services' in order to get the first two zungos built. Cary had to content himself with the knowledge that Borgu's trade had doubled in two years, and that fewer of the children who gathered round him in each village had pot bellies.

If Cary's improvements met with no recognition in Kaduna, they encountered actual hostility in Borgu itself. In an article entitled 'Policy for Aid', published in 1955, Cary recalled some of the objections raised by the Emir of Kaiama against the increase of trade in his kingdom. It was true that the people were richer, but they were also becoming insubordinate. Foreign traders passed through the district without paying courtesy calls, and as they went they spread alien ideas. Cary's progress was in fact his regress. 'He himself was a gentle, wise old man, deeply religious, and indulgent to his people; but he had the inescapable limitations of his age and education. And religion itself, the Mahommedan religion, meditative and world-rejecting, austere and puritanical, urged him to hate the new régime. If he had known the word, he would have called it materialistic.'

Nor were the village chiefs any more pleased than the Emir at Cary's developments. Their wives were now selling more produce to traders than ever before, and this meant they were neglecting their home duties. Village husbands were already aggrieved because Cary, in drawing up his code for the new native courts ('Justinian was left at the post'), laid down that no woman was to be compelled to stay with her husband against her will. The enforcement of this, which was extremely difficult as the husbands were usually members of the courts, did not result in more wives running away than in previous years; but the measure caused consternation, and Cary had to warn his successor in Borgu that it was not easy to get rid of what was in his view legalized slavery. And over and above this obscurantist response to his reforms, Cary suffered the irritation of knowing that the people for whom he was working extremely hard were convinced he was feathering his own nest and would eventually remove to England a large private fortune collected from the Borgawa. He was in fact unable to escape, whatever his actions, the fate of being an expatriate. As an expatriate poet has since ruefully put it:

> Feeling is no certificate
> One is ungainly
> And in it for gain.

3

'Life is a birthday present', Cary wrote in his Borgu diary; and though the entry is probably later than 1919, it captures the temper of his last tour in the division. It was one of the happiest periods of his life. Even when he could not interest either the Emir or the Secretariat in his schemes for developing Borgu, Cary could still find pleasure in his books and his writing. An account in his letters of a day's journey, on which everything went as wrong as it could, ends with Cary at last in camp (which meant, as often as not, a mud hut on a rubbish dump in the noisiest part of the village) reading Jane Austen and 'much soothed by her quiet wisdom'. This was unusual, for Cary did not in fact read many novels on this tour. He felt the need of more reflective works: among others, Hazlitt's *Table Talk*, Plutarch's *Morals*, Darwin's *Origin of Species*, Temple's *Essays* and the *Religio Medici* of Sir Thomas Browne. Browne's stately cadences were echoed in Cary's assessment reports in a way that must have surprised Kaduna.

Cary realized that the danger of working in complete isolation was that he was tempted to take to work as another man might take to drink. This awareness made him set a special value on the morning and evening rides he was sometimes able to enjoy when his trek took him along the banks of the Niger, away from the horizonless bush and the mental lianas of administration. The opening of *The Horse's Mouth*, Gulley Jimson's morning walk along the Embankment after his release from prison, perhaps owes something to Cary's memory of the sense of liberation these rides gave and the inventiveness they encouraged. For Cary was writing with a Jimson-like energy during the greater part of this last tour.

Some of this writing was in the form of aphorisms, apt to appear profound at one reading and platitudinous at another: 'Art should not aim at explaining life but making it worth living'; 'Art gives to man not sights, sounds and feelings, but eyes, ears and a heart'; 'The critic's duty is to find words for our sensations before a work of art – and sometimes to tell us where we ought to stand to see it in the best light'; 'Comedy springs from the likeness, tragedy from the difference, of human ineptitude'. Cary also started story after story on this tour; and though he finished very few of them, he had amassed, by May 1919, the manuscript equivalent of two and a half novels. The ease with which he wrote made production even on this scale a relaxation rather than an effort. 'I trot about all day when I'm not doing official work, chuckling over the situations I invent. I get more fun out of my books than any reader ever will' (6 September 1919).

At the same time, Cary was becoming increasingly aware that writing was to be for him a vocation and not a hobby. 'As a matter of fact, I have not even begun to find myself till this tour. Last tour was a re-beginning from the beginning and I burnt the whole batch. . . . I shan't burn this year's work. There are two unfinished novels I burn to get back to – I still take the keenest interest in them – and the one I am working at does not flag. So that in a year or two more, if there is no serious long interruption, I hope to do better

things' (9 August 1919). He owed this new confidence very largely
to his wife's hopes of him as a writer. In a letter of April 1919 he
speaks of the discouragement that his ambition had met with in the
past: 'the unsaid disbelief of others – the eagerness to push me into
some profession – the joy when I was found able to make money
like other people' (20 April 1919). Now he could be sure of a sympathetic reader for his day-to-day reports on the progress of his
stories. The difficulties he soon ran into made this sympathy especially valuable. For though Cary wrote easily, he was seldom satisfied
when he returned to what he had written, and already he was
developing the habit he was to retain all his life of rewriting each
episode four or five times. He did not as yet realize this method was
natural to him and tried instead to invent an elaborate scheme
for each novel and to keep to it in a steady start-to-finish pro-
gression. The whole trouble, he pointed out in another letter,
was that there was no system of apprenticeship in the writer's
craft:

> Writing is not like painting. The best way of learning painting is notori-
> ously to go and watch a big man paint. An hour of that is worth a week or
> a year of the art-schools. But one cannot see the novelist at work. Most
> of it is done in his head. Of course method one can learn. But where?
> No novelist has given a description of his method worth twopence. Each
> has to learn for himself. I am learning now. I am evolving a method.
>
> (21 May 1919)

In this process of trying to evolve a method Cary wrestled with two
problems which troubled him throughout his career as a writer.
One was the friction between plot and character: 'I make a plot –
get the characters moving – get to know them – and then I find
they are not evolving the plot – rather struggling with it' (19 May
1919). The other was the need for a personal style as the expression
of a personal vision. Cary was aware at this time of the danger
of his trying to see life through the spectacles of Conrad or of the
Russians, instead of using his own eyes. Perhaps his awareness of
this danger made him avoid reading contemporary novels during
this tour.

Although Cary's letters tell us a great deal about the technical pitfalls in the way of the novice storyteller, they say nothing about the themes and subject matter of the novels themselves. It is probable that one of the half-finished novels to which he meant to return later was the one called *Daventry*, which has an African setting. But towards the end of 1919 Cary complained how little material for observation was afforded him by Borgu. 'The stuff of writing as of painting is observation, but what can I see in Borgu? If I could see the black Borgawa I could write of them. But I can't. I see no more of them in their true lives than you do' (10 November 1919). In fact, Cary was not nearly so cut off from the Africans round him as these words suggest. But as his determination to become a professional writer grew, he felt increasingly the need to live in a complex society where he could study the behaviour of people whose cultural roots were the same as his own.

Yet Cary's letters of November 1919 give no indication that he intended to leave Nigeria. Two events decided that. The first occurred on his way home. Cary had sent some stories, avowedly pot-boilers, to an Oxford contemporary who had become a literary agent. When he was staying with a fellow official in Kontagora Province at the beginning of his long journey, Cary told his host that an editor in New York had accepted three of these stories and sent a cheque for £240 with a request for more information about the writer, whose style impressed him. And he added that if he was able to earn such a sum by three weeks' sparetime writing, he would do better in literature than on an Assistant District Officer's pay of barely five hundred a year.

Although these were false hopes, once Cary was back in England they weighed heavily in the balance against his return to Nigeria. What finally tipped the scale was a visit to the doctor. Cary suffered from asthma, which was exacerbated by the Northern Nigerian climate; and though his medical board in December 1919 described his health as 'fairly good', the doctor in England told him he ought not to return to the tropics. He accepted this advice and did not in fact see Africa again until twenty-three

years later. By that time he had published all of his novels
with an African setting as well as an eloquent plea for colonial
freedom.

7ᵗʰ December 1919 aetat. 31

Catching up with Africa
1943

I

In 1920, Joyce Cary and his wife bought the house in Oxford which was to be their permanent home; and here Cary began to write for a living. Difficult years followed. The Carys' small private income was drained away, in the post-war rise of prices, by the needs of their growing family. Financial crises were frequent, and each time one occurred Cary thought of returning to Africa; not to Nigeria, since the doctors had advised against that, but to another colony where his administrative experience would have secured him a good post. In the end he stuck to his career as a writer, largely because of his wife's unvarying trust and encouragement. Over ten years were to pass, however, before one of his novels, *Aissa Saved*, was accepted for publication.

There were two main causes of this delay. The first was that once Cary had stopped writing pot-boilers (as he had done, with the exception of a few stories sold to the *Strand Magazine* shortly after his return to England), the tales he wrote to his own standards did not please editors and publishers. The second was that even when Cary wrote to please himself, he failed to do so; novel after novel was cast aside without being submitted to any publisher. Later he was to sum up these attempts by saying, in a biographical note about himself: 'He also began to write books, but no sooner had he got half-way though a book than he perceived it was all nonsense: that is to say, an anecdote without significance or permanent value' (N85).

Cary's method as a novelist shows him to have been the kind of writer who had to see what he said before he knew what he meant.

He was amazingly inventive; throughout the twenties he crammed thick notebooks with sketches for characters and incidents, both factual and imaginary. From time to time he would rapidly write up something from one of these notebooks in the form of an episode. The next step was to scrutinize the episode to discover just why he had written it. The real pains of composition began here, as Cary wrested a significance out of what he had written, and repeatedly rewrote the piece in his effort to find the form that would be most expressive of that significance. 'It is not till the scene is complete that the writer can assume a new role, as critic, and man of ideas, to judge his own work. He is the only man who can judge it at this stage, for he alone can know what he was trying to convey. And it is now that he needs a clear picture of his world, for he has to ask himself "Is this what I mean?" Unless he knows what he means he cannot devise a form. For meaning is form' ('Form and Meaning').

Cary had no such clear pictures of his world when he began to write in earnest in the twenties; and without it he could not find the underlying significance of his fragmentary writings and so re-shape them into a novel which would meet the standard set by his own reading of Hardy, James, Conrad and the Russians. Each incident as he wrote it appeared meaningless, without relation to any total view of experience. 'I was stuck for years', he recalled towards the end of his life. 'I was stuck for more years than I realized myself; it was nearly ten years. I wrote a lot of stuff, but it's all in the attic. And the thing that held me up all the time, was the want of a satisfactory general idea' ('The Novelist at Work').

Cary thus set off in quest of a personal philosophy which would give meaning to his experiences and enable him to cast them into that form without which his instincts as an artist would have remained unsatisfied. This meant that the years of unsuccessful writing were also years of successful reading. Cary was lucky in having the Bodleian Library almost at his door. He began systematically to explore questions in philosophy of which he had been half-aware since his undergraduate days. Metaphysics took him to religion, religion to psychology. And alongside his curiosity about the individual mind went a concern, quickened by his political experience, with man as a social being. He not only read a great deal of political theory, but he began also to discover the revolutionary theories of the post-war anthropologists.

His African experiences were also subjected, during the intellectual turbulence of the inter-war years, to repeated scrutiny in the light of the discussions which went on everywhere – in books and pamphlets, in pubs and common rooms and parliamentary lobbies – on the rights and wrongs of colonialism. The political principles by which the Empire had been ruled since the days of Joseph Chamberlain were under continual fire in the nineteen-twenties and thirties. After the publication of *The Dual Mandate* in 1922, many writers who shared Lugard's belief that the resources of the tropical countries ought to be developed by the colonial powers for the mutual benefit of the indigenous population and of the industrialized West, began to question if that development was in fact taking place in territories such as Nigeria. Among these critics were many former administrators. They ranged from Sir Donald Cameron, who was shocked, on his return to Nigeria as Governor in 1931, by the way the country had been allowed to stagnate in the twenties, to the former District Officer who wrote in 1936: 'It is not possible to put one's finger on a single contribution or new idea or new development in the administration of the policy of Indirect Rule since Lugard's time.'[1] It certainly looks, from this short perspective of time, as if Lugard's immediate successors in Nigeria were chiefly concerned to preserve, and even extend, the powers of a number of picturesque medieval monarchs. One of Cary's first colleagues, J. F. J. Fitzpatrick, stated in 1924 that before the coming of the British the autocracy of an Emir was at least 'tempered with assassination'; now, with the whole authority of the suzerain power to back him up, he could do just as he pleased. If it pleased him to be both corrupt and despotic, he could often rely on his faults going unnoticed, or at least unnoted, by the British administrator on the spot, who was

[1] W. R. Crocker: *Nigeria: A Critique of British Colonial Administration*, p. 216.

sometimes all too ready to be impressed by the ruler's courtly dignity. Other critics pointed out that this cult of the Emirs implicated the British in the support of an alien ruling caste, the Fulani; and that it resulted in official support being lent in any dispute to the Moslem against the pagan, and to Islam against Christianity.

All these might be called short-view criticisms. They came from writers who, while they admired Lugard's practical wisdom in seeking to develop the country along the people's own lines, complained that it was not in fact being so developed. But alongside these strictures there grew up, in the inter-war period, a body of criticism which was based on a longer view, a view implied in a definition of indirect rule by A. V. Murray: ' "Indirect Rule" has reference in Africa to a situation which includes black and white with the white on top, but where the institutions of the black are not abolished but "progressively" adapted to modern conditions.'[1] One day the tropical dependencies would be independent. What then would be the value to them of an administrative system which assumed that the whites would always be on top? Lugard had in fact maintained that one of the merits of his system of indirect rule was that if at any time the British had to withdraw the country would be left with an adequate working system of government. But he was thinking of such a withdrawal in terms of military or economic necessity, and not as the prologue to the creation of an independent modern state. Historically, it was almost impossible for anyone of Lugard's generation to conceive of a tropical Africa in which the whites would not be on top. Events in India in the nineteen-twenties helped, however, to bring the notion of self-governing African democracies within the grasp of most liberal-minded English people. Consequently English writers in the thirties began to attack the principles of indirect rule from much the same standpoint as that adopted by American critics and the educated African minority on the West Coast: the standpoint of national self-determination.

There were various lines of attack. First it was argued that feudal

[1] A. V. Murray: *The School in the Bush* (2nd ed., 1936), p. 402.

chieftaincies could not be incorporated into a modern state; and indeed, one of the chief opponents of Nigerian nationalism, Lugard's immediate successor Clifford, said so with considerable satisfaction in 1920, when he described the attempt to weld Nigeria into a nation as 'a deadly blow . . . at the very root of national self-government in Nigeria, which secures to each separate people the right to maintain its identity, its individuality, and nationality, its chosen form of government'.[1] Then there was the argument that Lugard and his successors, in their educational policy, had tried to perpetuate the power of the ruling class and had kept knowledge from the mass of the people. To a critic such as A. V. Murray, who knew a chief's power in Africa to be a social contract rather than a hereditary right, British eagerness to give a public-school education to the sons of chiefs suggested that these future rulers were being trained to use their power, not for their people, but against them; and the hostility of many administrators to Christian missions was traced to a fear that the westernized African would not fit easily into the feudal organization of an Emirate, but would rather become an agitator – or liberator – clamouring for democracy.

The official reply to critics who deplored the lack of popular education in the North of Nigeria and of higher education anywhere in the country was that the country's resources would not stretch to meet these needs. This in its turn provided the long-view critics of indirect rule with another line of attack. Nigeria, it was said, ought to have financial help from the metropolitan country. At the present time, when it is axiomatic that fully-developed countries (from whatever motive) help underdeveloped ones, it is easy to forget that at the beginning of this century the belief that colonies should be self-supporting was no less axiomatic. 'When the British Government in 1929 opened the Colonial Development Fund, it began a policy so different in conception from those which had, up till then, disposed its relations with the African peoples, that I am not very sure it has yet realized or faced the consequences.

[1] Quoted by James S. Coleman: *Nigeria: Background to Nationalism* (1958), p. 197.

Partly because the new departure, like the source of a great river at
the top of a watershed, was a small stream. It was seen only long
afterwards to belong to a different line of country.' So Joyce Cary
himself wrote in 1946, in *Britain and West Africa* (pp. 64-5). The
reason why few grasped the revolutionary nature of this financial
aid was that for many years it remained the merest trickle. The 1931
slump not only put grants in aid out of the question, but by its
adverse effects on Nigeria's overseas trade brought about a twenty
per cent. cut in public spending. And as soon as Britain had recovered from the depression sufficiently to pursue a policy of financial
aid, the 1939 war put a stop to all developments. Such governmental change of heart as existed was difficult to detect during the
thirties and early forties; and left-wing attacks on colonial *laisser
faire* and stagnation were particularly vigorous during these decades.

2

During the nineteen-thirties and forties, Joyce Cary was an active
member of the Liberal Party. The party's Committee, early in the
war, asked him to write a small book on African colonialism for the
Liberal Book Club. Cary had by that time written five novels
wholly or partly set in Nigeria, and had decided not to set any more
novels in Africa, so there was no danger of the proposed book
having a stultifying effect on his imagination; and he undertook the
commission the more gladly because it gave him a chance to correct
false notions about his views on Africa, the result of some careless
reviews of his novels.

The Case for African Freedom, published in July 1941, appeared in
an enlarged edition in 1944. In the Introduction to this second
edition Cary disclaims any right to speak as an authority on African
affairs:

> I do not write as an African expert who has given his life to African
> problems, but as a man who, in his African service, made mistakes, who

afterwards reflected on that experience and its meaning; who, after ten years of active, thoughtless and various experience in the world began, rather late in youth, to ask himself what it amounted to; to dig up all his foundations, to find out exactly what they were; who discovered then, as you might expect, that some of them were mud, some were hollow caves of air, others sand; and who then slowly and painfully rebuilt them, as far as he could manage the task, as a coherent whole, on which to found a new life and a new mind.

(p. 12)

The phrase 'a coherent whole' used here is an important reminder that Cary's views on Africa as he developed them between the wars in his African novels were not merely the intellectual drift of the period. The political climate of Oxford in the thirties certainly helped to move the current of his thoughts in the direction they were taking; but his reflections on colonialism, if they were to have any validity for him at all, had to be related to that 'satisfying general idea' which he had sought ever since his retirement from Nigeria, and which had become more clearly defined in each successive novel up to *Mister Johnson*.

This satisfactory general idea, the basis of Cary's thinking, is that freedom, which is the inescapable human lot, constitutes a 'field of power'. This is the theme of *Power in Men* (1940), Cary's first political book, which is an austerely presented critique of the nineteenth-century concept of liberty as absence of restraint; it redefines social liberty in positive terms as an enlargement of the individual's scope for creative action. The whole argument of *The Case for African Freedom* is for an extension to the African people of this freedom as power: the individual power to conceive a fuller life, which education could give; the power to labour and multiply, which health services could promote; and the power to build, through financial and technical aid, the full modern economy which was the necessary foundation of a democratic political system. The deep differences between the two concepts of freedom, the permissive and the dynamic, was summed up for Cary in the remark of an old chief he had known on the Dahomey frontier. The chief had been told that he was free to exercise his powers as a traditional ruler. But when he closed a trade route across the frontier and nearly caused an international incident, he found himself overruled by the suzerain power and bitterly complained that he felt like a slave.

I did not understand the force of this old man's bitter complaint. I thought it was enough to say, 'I give you freedom to act; carry on.' I did not realize his feelings when he discovered that what he thought was a reasonable act, was to me stupid and wrong. In fact his complaint, that he felt like a slave, was not a piece of petulance, as I supposed, but one of those sayings in which a very simple man of honest feelings penetrates in one stroke to the heart of the matter.

He meant that it was not much good telling an old man to take his freedom, if he could not understand the new order. He merely tumbled into humiliation. . . .

The whole conception of producing freedom by a sudden political act belongs to a school of thought which never did face the root problem of liberty; which did actually believe, or try to believe, that Robinson Crusoe had more liberty than an ordinary British or American citizen. To make a man free you have to create a whole social order of a special kind: the democratic.

(pp. 24-5)

Soon after the publication of *The Case for African Freedom*, Joyce Cary had the opportunity to test this concept of freedom, evolved largely from his reflections upon his early Nigerian experiences, against new and wider experience of Africa. In January 1943 he left England for East Africa, where he hoped to get up-to-date material for a film script which he had undertaken to write at the request of the Ministry of Information. 'It is, you understand, not to be a propaganda film', he wrote to Edwardes, 'but a full-size story film with a background showing, by the way, the administration at work' (21 October 1943). Unfortunately, the semi-official colouring of the undertaking is to be felt everywhere in the script of *Men of Two Worlds*, and the dialogue is overlaid with that schoolmasterly tone peculiar to most productions of the wartime Ministry of Information. The fact that it was a commissioned work seems to have deprived it of the vitality which informs Cary's other African stories. The central theme, the difficulties confronting the educated African when he returns to help his own people, repeats that of *The African Witch*. Many of the characters, too, are borrowed from Cary's African novels, and do not survive the transplantation. An exception is the District Officer, Rendall, perhaps because he is Cary's own spokesman when he urges that more Africans be given positions of responsibility: 'It's a job that an African could do better than a European. It takes years for a man of one race to gain real understanding of another. An African has twenty years' start on any European, however willing and able.' In spite of these shortcomings, *Men of Two Worlds* might have had great documentary interest, for the location chosen by Cary (who did not return for the actual making of the film) was the slopes of Mount Kilimanjaro, and the local people played prominent roles. Unfortunately, the only copy of these sequences was lost in transit to America, and the film that the public eventually saw was mainly a studio production.

But, from Joyce Cary's own point of view, the journey was anything but a waste of time, for it showed him a quite different Africa from that which he had known in the First World War. He first travelled by sea to Freetown, where Graham Greene, at that time stationed there with M.I.6, lent him a Nissen hut in which he continued writing *The Horse's Mouth* until it was time to fly on to Lagos. This was Cary's first experience of Nigeria's capital city. In 1914, when the unification of Nigeria was still only a paper fact, political officers of the Northern service had gone straight from the ship to the train without seeing the capital at all. Now Cary found Lagos an exciting place. The fact that he was trying at the time to see the world through the eyes of Gulley Jimson perhaps helped him to enjoy its brilliant colour and the bounce and bustle of its inhabitants. In any case, this visit dispelled all Cary's old Northern prejudices against the upstarts of the Coast. 'You may like it or you may hate it', he wrote of the ferment of life in the Lagos streets, 'but it is the direct result of setting free those energies which have made the modern world and will remake it again pretty often in the next few million years. It is real individual freedom getting its head loose and throwing out its front legs.' Even the 'yellow Press' of Lagos, which had so exasperated Lugard, now delighted Cary as a symptom of this freedom:

> It has newspapers which not only criticize the Government but, what is much more significant, appeal to a public which takes a much keener interest in its own private affairs than official announcements of any kind. Of course in any old civilized country people are used to the local newspaper. They quite expect to find the front page given up to local scandals; and what we might call world news, even war news, crowded into a side column, or the second page. But such newspapers, run by Africans for Africans, are not common in Africa. And they are a very important symptom of freedom in a people, *real* freedom; that is, individual and independent development.

('Article on Africa')

When he flew on to Uganda, Cary felt at once the difference between what was now to him real freedom – that is, freedom as power – and the permissive and negative freedom of a people whose tribal life was as yet little touched by Western ideas. He found an exception among the Chaggas of Tanganyika, whose co-operatives (he told Edwardes) had opened his eyes. But he contrasted both Uganda and Northern Nigeria, to their disadvantage, with Lagos. Clean streets and public transport in Kampala were no compensation for a lack of political and intellectual vitality; and Northern Nigeria was 'still pretty much of an official turnout, a smart show-piece. . . . Of course, it has schools and hospitals, all very nice and clean and useful, but the real life of the people is still almost untouched. They jog along in the twelfth century or thereabouts, an anachronism, though very nice to look at' ('Article on Africa').

Cary attributed this difference to one thing: the widespread use of English in Southern Nigeria. In the North of Nigeria and in East Africa the use of English was discouraged, and the *lingua franca* was an African language. Cary returned from his African tour of 1943 convinced that English as a second language was a liberating force. This view, of course, challenged a principle of indirect rule; if a people were to develop 'along their own lines', the vernacular had to be preserved and encouraged. As no one at the beginning of the century thought of the lines going very far, no one bothered very much about the fact that a man who could speak only Hausa or Swahili was cut off from the whole of Western thought and technology. But by 1943 the extent of that deprivation was only too plain to Cary as he travelled through East Africa. A year later he was still angry enough about it to write that the African was 'getting our cheap clothes, our cheap songs, our popular music, our mass slogans, or mass produced pots and knives and furniture, and he is not getting our magnificent art or science or literature or philosophy. . . . If we give a full European civilization to Africa, we won't get a Europe in Africa. Africa will still be Africa and have its own culture' (N85).

3

Everything Cary saw on his 1943 visit to Nigeria, Uganda, and Tanganyika confirmed his belief that the freedom of modern democratic life must be extended to Africa. In consequence, this theme is even more persuasively stated in the second edition of *The Case for African Freedom* than it had been in the first. It is also the basis of the small book, *Britain and West Africa*, which Cary wrote for Longmans in 1946, and of several articles on colonial affairs published in American periodicals.

Cary did not share the sense of guilt which is commonly found among critics of colonialism. He viewed the race for Africa which took place between 1874 and 1900 as a historical phenomenon, the inevitable expression of the times' popular imperialism in all its forms – nationalistic, romantic, and evangelical. He went further and stated that 'European conquest with all its faults has brought incomparably more good than harm to Africa'. It was true that there had been grave abuses of colonial power, especially when the new imperialism of annexation replaced the old trading imperialism of the eighteenth and early nineteenth centuries. Traders had been compelled to deal fairly with the local people in order to preserve their goodwill; concessionaires were able to enforce labour on their own terms. Yet even the worst results of the partition of Africa were to Cary's thinking less terrible than the Arab slave raids in the East and the Fulani slave raids in the West, which were living memories to many Africans at the time that he wrote.

> Talk of the white man's burden is now a joke. Probably it is good that it should be a joke, for it was too easily used to cover a mean complacence and to breed that hypocrisy which of all vices most quickly corrupts a nation. But the responsibility of Britain towards her dependants was not a joke to the Whigs who impeached Hastings; to the men who fought the slave trade; to the Church people who have always supported the missions; nor to a thousand humble officials in the British service whose duty, as they were taught, was to the African people.
>
> (*Britain and West Africa*, p. 48)

The sense of history which enabled Cary to deal fairly and objectively with the early stages of a contact that has produced all too much lurid and even hysterical description also enabled him to see that, by the nineteen-forties, both the new imperialism of the nineties and the early twentieth-century concept of trusteeship had had their day. By the time of the Second World War, a drastic change in colonial policy was needed. Indeed, the war itself, by bringing African troops into contact with European ones and with the life of Asian and European cities, increased the pressure for change. And to the internal pressure of racial grievance there was added the external pressure of what Cary calls the moral sense of humanity. The acceleration of social change in Britain in the nineteen-forties added further urgency to Cary's appeal. 'Great changes will happen in any case; good or bad. Time is short to make them good.'

The vital first step to freedom as Cary understood it was to find all possible means of raising the standard of living throughout the continent. Political liberty, he insisted, was no use to a starving man; it came at the end and not the beginning of a people's emancipation. But in Africa the economic reformer inevitably met with two forms of resistance. One was from the land itself. Africa was not the cornucopia dreamt up by late Victorian journalists. On the contrary, it was desperately poor. Cary's first experience of Nigeria had been of an area stricken by famine. His 1943 journey showed him that Africa's vegetation was still being burnt and grazed away and its topsoil still being blown into the desert or washed into the sea.

These physical obstacles to Africa's progress could not be over-stated, because stating them drew attention to the magnitude of the help required. The political resistance was less serious: the resistance of the racialist who thought the African was not good enough for civilization, and of the sentimentalist who thought civilization was not good enough for him. In fact, Cary did not trouble to argue with the racialist; affectionate memories of Tasuki inventing his multiple pulley, and even the sedate Mr Graves quelling a riot single-handed in Kaiama, were enough to refute the suggestion that the master-race had any monopoly of intelligence and initiative. But Cary had to admit that he had once shared the paternal and protective feeling of those who thought the African was too good for civilization. When he had seen a Tula tribesman enter the Niger Company store at Nafada and transform himself from 'a warrior fit for the Parthenon into a nigger minstrel' he had felt that such people would be freer and happier if they could be protected from a cash economy. The pressures of history, however, were all against the creation of human nature reserves. The tribes were disbanding of their own free will – or more exactly, wills, since the drive towards freedom came from the individuals; and modern science, in disturbing the balance between population and sub-sistence, was forcing the pace of social change as the only means of survival.

It was possible to see the system of indirect rule as one outcome of this British tribalistic sentiment which was more concerned to preserve indigenous institutions than to develop the country's resources in the direction of a complex modern state. Cary's 1943 journey certainly quickened his impatience with many aspects of indirect rule, and in a notebook entry written after his return he summed up the system's rationale, or lack of it, as 'Let the cabbages grow their own way and kill their own weeds and bring themselves to market' (N85). But by the time he came to revise *The Case for*

African Freedom he was able to get the colonial policy of trusteeship once more into perspective. This was a remarkable feat, since he had been well indoctrinated with that policy in his days as a colonial administrator. Now, twenty-five years later, he was able to pass beyond mere repudiation to a position from which he could evaluate indirect rule as the natural product of ideas of government which had prevailed in the nineteenth century, and still dominated British local government in the twentieth. 'The conception was rooted first in legal security against violence, then in the old idea of liberty as an absence of restraint, and finally in self-development within local resources.' Then, in the period between the wars, a new conception of the State gave rise to the belief that the government, far from leaving the individual to his own devices, ought to increase his freedom of action by social legislation. 'What has happened is not that the life-work of great government servants like Lord Lugard has become worthless; but that the point of view from which all government is judged has suddenly changed. Critics no longer ask of a government, "Have you protected the religious liberty and respected the native institutions, as far as possible, of your dependent peoples?" but "What have you done to raise the standard of living, of health and education in your colonies?"' (*The Case for African Freedom*, p. 57).

Given that it was anachronistic to judge the success of indirect rule by the criteria of the mid-twentieth century, it might still be judged by its own standards: had it, in fact, enabled colonial peoples to develop along their own lines? Cary had to admit that in some areas, notably the North of Nigeria, it had failed to do so. It had even paralysed social development by strengthening the autocratic powers of the chiefs. Lugard, he reminded his readers, warned his District Officers against this in his *Political Memoranda*, where he laid it down that native institutions were to be improved and not stereotyped. But he had had to contend with an innate English romanticism: 'The tourist mind is not uncommon among officials. I had it myself, that love of the picturesque which invites the traveller to delight in anything unfamiliar and racy of the soil; in national government, native costume, native dances; national religious ceremony, even national dirt and poverty, so long as it is different from what he can see at home' (*The Case for African Freedom*, p. 63). Provided, however, that this kind of stagnation could be avoided, there was no reason in Cary's opinion why the machinery of indirect rule, which had been devised to serve the ends of Edwardian trusteeship, should not be turned over to the service of colonial development directed towards the Welfare State. For one thing, the difference between direct and indirect rule had been overstressed; except in the largest Nigerian Emirates and in the Kingdom of Buganda in East Africa, the central government had always exercised a great deal of its authority directly through District Commissioners. For another, local self-government as it had been fostered by indirect rule could be a powerful help to development. Local enterprises, undertaken through the initiative of local teachers, dispensers, agricultural assistants, could capture villagers' interests in a way that the best-laid plans of a stranger, whether African or expatriate, could never hope to do.

So social change could come inside the framework of indirect rule provided that there were sufficient means for an attack to be made on all the fields of deficiency at once. Education remained a mockery while children were debilitated by fever and parasites; health services depended for their effect on wider education, or people would go on washing in water infested with guinea-worm; education was needed before farming methods could be improved; there had to be better crops before children would be well enough nourished to benefit from their schooling. And although most reforms, given the economic and technical aid required, could be carried out within the existing political structure, reforms were needed in the administration: better communications between the Secretariat and the District Officer in the bush, to prevent the latter degenerating into a well-known colonial type, the office deadhead; more opportunities for the bush officer to travel in order to see the way things were done in other parts of Africa, or to attend refresher courses in Europe.

There was nothing very original in suggestions such as these at the time Cary made them. It could even be said that other writers made them more systematically; and the better reviewers in 1944 were justified in complaining about the garrulity of *The Case for African Freedom*. The book suffered from being the revision of comments made before Cary had revisited Africa and reordered his ideas on colonialism. It also suffered, as the summary here attempted shows, from divided aims. Cary was afraid that his argument for a new approach to African problems might be taken as a reflection on the work of the men he most admired. In consequence, the book yokes uncomfortably together a call to action for the future with a justification of the past. The new edition was dedicated to Edwardes and Carlyle; and Cary sent a copy of the first edition to Edwardes with a written inscription and a covering letter 'to express my gratitude and respect to you who at the very beginning of my too short time in the service put me in the right way of approach to the African and my responsibilities in Nigeria; and gave me, I think, much of the enthusiasm which carried me forward in the next years. I wish I could celebrate fittingly all that glorious band of the Nigerian pioneers – perhaps I shall try another day' (26 July 1941). The same wish to defend and justify 'a great generation of public servants' confuses Cary's articles on Africa intended for American readers. *Britain and West Africa*, in contrast, is a single-minded book. Cary was writing for what publishers now term the sixth-form public in both Britain and West Africa, and therefore felt no need to grind his axe. The book's chronological scheme enabled him to give Carlyle's generation its due meed of praise and then to go on to explain and champion the new policies of colonial development and welfare to which the 1945 government was committed. It is a good book which could with advantage be brought up to date; the 'future' of Cary's last chapter is our immediate past.

This brings us to what is likely to be the first reaction of a present-day reader to Cary's political writings on Africa. They have dated. The acceleration of which he spoke has continued, making Cary's 1944 views on Africa as much part of the past to us as Lugard's were to him. An example is his advocacy of 'a full European culture' for Africa. This belief of the most progressive thinkers of the forties produced the African university colleges with their departments of Classics and ground plans modelled on Cambridge. Only a decade later the demand was for independent African universities which should have as one of their most important functions the study and preservation of African culture. Joyce Cary was himself later affected by this change; his introduction to Denys Craig's novel, *Man in Ebony*, published in 1950, is a plea to Africans to explore their own religion and give it literary expression before it is overwhelmed by Islam and Christianity: 'A people without a literature does not even know itself and cannot be known to history.'

The aspect of *The Case for African Freedom* which most dates it today is its insistence that economic development is the necessary prelude to political independence. In fact, this view was already being outmoded between 1941 and 1944, as Cary indicates in his apologetic preface to the second edition, where he refers to political freedom as the led horse of his campaign. It could, of course, be argued – though I do not think Cary himself would have argued that way – that in seeking first the political kingdom Kwame Nkrumah has not given freedom, as Cary understood the term, to Ghana; and that events in the Congo in 1960 justified his belief that 'power should be handed over gradually so that native responsibility increases at about equal speed with economic and political development'. Right or wrong, Cary's insistence on food before votes has become as irrelevant as his concern with the rival merits of direct and indirect rule. In tropical Africa, colonial rule, with all its accompanying anxieties about how and when power should be transferred to the subject people, is a thing of the past.

Finally, *The Case for African Freedom* is out of date because the case itself is won. Although it will be many decades before aid and development achieve a freedom from want comparable with the freedom from fear that was the greatest achievement of the old colonialism, public opinion in Britain and America recognizes the vital need to Africa of Cary's kind of freedom. And when one has said this, one has given *The Case for African Freedom* the highest praise possible for a piece of controversial writing. To borrow Cary's own aphorism from the book, nothing fails like success. His plea, joined to that of other liberal writers of his generation, has succeeded so well that we no longer need to listen to it.

But if Cary's political writings on Africa are thus honourably outdated as propaganda, they retain a high interest for the reader of his novels, particularly those with an African setting. Like these novels, his political writings interpret past experiences in the light of a personal philosophy which it had taken Cary upward of a decade to evolve. In *The Case for African Freedom*, freedom is presented as the individual's power to create his own world, his own sphere of power and glory; and, just as in the novels, this creative force keeps meeting the immovable obstacles of the physical, 'given' world and of those rigid social conventions which are themselves the petrified creative force of a past generation. The results of the impact are presented to us in the novels (where matters are made yet more complicated by the conflict of personal visions in marriage and family life) as themes for tragic or comic contemplation; we are invited to share Cary's interpretation of life, but not to act upon it. The political writings, however, call for action: the action of breaking down the obstacles against which personal freedom so often strikes and founders in Africa.

A sight which moved Cary deeply when he travelled in Africa in 1943 was a shy group of girls in a dark school corridor. The first girls in that community to receive any education, they were the daughters of Moslem parents who had sent them to school voluntarily and at their own expense. Looking at them, Cary could feel the barriers breaking. The barriers in this case were those of prejudice and apathy; elsewhere they were barriers of hunger and disease. The energy of a really creative vision was needed if scope was ever to be made for the individual African to live his own life. 'Life more abundant' is a favourite phrase with the West African politician, and the cynical English administrator has often complained that this means bigger and spikier Cadillacs every year for the politician and his immediate friends. Cary was not only free from such cynicism, but could respond sympathetically and positively to the wish for life more abundant. A woman education officer of Cary's generation, who brought together in Northern Nigeria just such a group of Moslem girls as those Cary describes, has said that the experience of teaching them was that of seeing the first movement of the spirit on the face of the waters. The creation image defines the meaning such an experience had for Cary also. In the wish for the multiplication table or a Manchester cloth or a Cadillac he recognized (as he said in the Preface to the Carfax edition of *The African Witch*) the determination of all people 'to create some glory and dignity for themselves and those they love'. A profound delight in such creative freedom of spirit gives force to Cary's political arguments, as it gives vitality to his novels.

Fiction

The Approach to a Story

I

During the last few years of his life, Joyce Cary explained his aims and methods as a novelist in many articles and broadcasts. These were not undertaken in self-defence against the reviewers, uncomprehending as their notices often were. In fact, he told the American critic, Mark Schorer, that he was anxious not to enlighten the reviewer or thesis-writer at the cost of alienating the ordinary reader:

> I do not want to start by saying 'this novel is a metaphysical construction based on a comprehensive idea of life' or they will stop entering into my characters' lives and instead treat the book, if they tackle it at all, as a kind of cross-word puzzle – they will imagine an allegory. And I detest allegory – my people are real people in a real world or they are nothing.
>
> (13 October 1951)

For the same reason, Cary found satisfaction in the fact that critics considered his books to be over-objective and formless. This meant that he had succeeded in concealing both their metaphysics and their construction. He also resisted the temptation to write a general introduction to his works, which he would have liked to call 'The Comedy of Freedom'. But anxious as he was to avoid self-justification, Cary also remembered how he had had to learn the novelist's craft by years of trial and error, and felt, as a master craftsman, he could save young writers from some, at least, of the errors. Others might learn from his experience, as art students could learn from watching an old hand at work on the canvas.

In all his accounts of the creative process, Cary distinguishes three stages: intuition, approach, and form. By intuition Cary means something more than sympathy or insight. Rather, it is an imaginative leap into a character's situation at a moment of tragic or comic crisis. All his books were, he admitted, about someone in a jam. An article called 'Form and Meaning' develops this idea.

> One writes a dialogue, a scene, by a process that has to be called intuition, for want of a more precise term. This is to say, it is not a logical or rational process. It is more like empathy. It is no good asking oneself 'How would this fellow act now, how would he speak?' Nothing could be more frustrating. Characters in the imagination, like characters in actual life, begin to fade, to melt at the edges, the moment one tries to analyse them. One does not invent their speech, one knows how they would speak before they begin. Perhaps it is not far from the truth to say that for the moment one is that character. In dialogue that means a change of being every few seconds, and though judgement is not wholly crowded out, though there is still a critical self somewhere murmuring 'All this is off the point, X is breaking out in a new way, he will have to be subdued or he will pull the book out of shape,' yet its voice is small and weak among the noise and action and conversation.

When the imaginative hubbub has subsided, the still small voice of judgement gets a hearing, as it begins to analyse and explore the theme which has been intuitively presented. The novelist has now to ask himself, 'Just why did I write that?'

> Now that is where what I call the approach begins. Because an experience of any kind belongs to a mass of impressions, feelings which are very complex, including fundamental emotional values. I mean universal values belonging to a fundamental reality, and also private subjective elements, prejudices, misunderstandings, and very likely subconscious motives. So you have to examine it closely before you give it form, or it will falsify you or you will falsify it.
>
> ('The Approach, the Formal Construction, the Style')

At this point, the point at which the writer stands back and asks himself what he means, Cary believed he would be lost if he had no clear personal philosophy to help him to interpret his intuition. When, in 1950, he first described the intellectual approach which a writer needed to make to his intuitions, Cary appears to have considered the intuition itself as a pure 'yarn', of the kind he sketched out in his notebooks in the twenties; something which had to wait for the formulation of his personal philosophy before he could give it narrative form. But on reflection Cary seems to have realized that intuitions are themselves pre-selected in accordance with a writer's total vision. In so far as freedom became the central concern of Cary's thought, all his published novels emanated from his concept of freedom. Even when characters and events in them had a basis in fact, those particular characters and events were sifted out of other memories because they lent themselves to his general theme. Yet each character in a jam retained his or her inexplicable tendency to do unexpected things; if the judgement made an informing approach to the intuition, the intuition often retaliated by stretching and shaking the form imparted to it by the judgement. The result as Cary said, was a highly complex equation: 'the form of the book affects the form of the character who must, all the same, develop according to the laws of its own being as well as the writer's' ('Speaking of Books').

When Cary says firmly 'I would not dream of choosing a method, or a form, or a style until I knew exactly what the book was about and what it had to do' ('The Approach, the Formal Construction, the Style'), he knows he is describing, not the end of the writer's struggle, but a further phase of it. For even after the writer has reflected on his intuition to the point of recognizing its significance to himself as an individual holding a certain view of life, and has chosen the form which seems most expressive of the theme thus evolved, he is still apt to find new tensions developing between form and theme. The sequences of unheeding violence in *Aissa Saved*, for example, were at one time interrupted by a good deal of what Cary called 'Russian colloquy' between the administrator's short views and the missionary's long ones. This had to go because it did not fit in with the form of the novel that Cary was writing. Another struggle between form and meaning led to the repeated re-writings of *Prisoner of Grace*. Cary was dissatisfied with Nina as narrator, tried the third-person approach, then dropped that for a 'false first', or neutral narrator's viewpoint. Finally he hit on the device of Nina's parentheses which enabled him to make the narrative sound like her authentic voice without at the same time giving the impression that she was 'telling on' her husband. Instead, she gives him – and herself – away in her asides.

By the time he wrote the script 'The Approach, the Formal Construction, the Style', Cary could draw on thirty years of experience as a novelist. The talk is outstandingly interesting for the light it throws on many aspects of his writing: on, for example, his repetitions, which have been frequently criticized. Cary justifies them as the inevitable result of a writer's contemplation of his subject, enabling him to give a depth and richness to its development comparable with a composer's varied repetition and development of a theme through the movement of a symphony. Another of Cary's practices as a novelist which he justifies in the same script, calling Dostoevsky to his support, is that of putting into his characters' mouths inexplicable phrases which are seen in retrospect, and after the character has been given time to develop, to reveal very complex states of mind.

These, however, were refinements of technique which Cary developed over the years. We are concerned here with his beginnings as a novelist; and it is interesting to see that in his very earliest attempts he encountered the two great difficulties which he stresses again and again in his mature reflections on his craft: the effort to understand fully, in the light of his total experience, the intuitions which came to him with such compelling vividness; and the effort to cast his narrative into a form (setting and characters, tone and style) which, by achieving a perfect union of *sens* with *matière*, would be fully and justly expressive of his theme. When Cary abandoned a book it was nearly always for the reason that one or other of these struggles – to find the meaning in the matter, or to give the matter a form which would bring out the meaning – had proved too much for him. Two works written before the nineteen-thirties, but never published, are worth attention for the way they illustrate this struggle. One of them, a short novel called *Daventry*, is complete in only a skeletal way; the other, *Cock Jarvis*, runs to about a million words and exists in a huge pile of fragments.

2

Cary's handwriting, in the manuscript of *Daventry*, is identical with that of his letters from Borgu; and *Daventry* is almost certainly the novel written in Africa under Conrad's influence to which he referred in an interview in 1954 (*Writers at Work*, p. 61). The story is based on an incident in Cary's second tour in Nigeria. On 13 September 1916 he wrote to his wife that he was expecting to leave the garrison at Lokoja to ride on a patrol to Muri Province, where an Assistant District Officer called Maltby had been killed by pagan tribesmen: 'West found his skull wrapped up in his burberry in the Montal juju house.' Although someone else went in the end, the incident roused a kind of intuitive sympathy in Cary, who was soon to return to work similar to Maltby's: 'Poor Maltby ought never to have been in Montal without an escort.'

The Montals or Montols (actually, the Tel; the prefix means 'we are') were a notoriously truculent group; but they had been comparatively quiet for some years and had even paid their taxes. In July 1916 Maltby elected to visit them without an escort of police, in order to collect some arrears of tax. He took with him an Ankwe chief called Rapman, who had somewhat nominal authority over the Montols, and other leading members of the native administration, including two Political Agents. Maltby forbade the party to carry any arms whatsoever. This gesture of trust failed; the Montols fell on the whole party, killing fifty-nine of them. A punitive expedition marched into the district, inflicted almost as many casualties on the Montols, and found and buried Maltby's remains.

Cary based his story on the last few days of Maltby's life. *Daventry* is sent into the pagan district of Weji by his District Officer, Crompton, who wants him to win the tribe's confidence and start building a road. He warns him against over-enthusiastic mapping by recalling the fate of a tin-prospector who entered the area to survey it – a cross-reference to a real event of 1913. Daventry declines the offer of a police escort and takes with him, besides his carriers, only the Political Agent, Audu, the usual European's retinue of cook, small boy and horse-boy, and the chief from the settled part of Weji, who is called Langa – obviously a recollection of Rapman's title of the Long Kemai. At first all goes well and Daventry enjoys the climb up to the plateau. But panic seizes the party when they enter a deserted village where the warm hearths reveal that the inhabitants are in hiding. Daventry, however, refuses to turn back. The party is ambushed by pagans with poisoned arrows. Langa is killed outright; the remnant, including Daventry, Audu and the servants, begins the retreat during which the cook dies of terror and the rest of their poisoned wounds – with the exception of the horse-boy, Ibrahim, who leaves Daventry to die on the floor of the rest-house in Langa's village. Daventry's slow withdrawal, a structural necessity to the story, is made possible by the nature of the attack, and although this did not fit with the facts of the Maltby case, Cary could find ample precedent for it in stories of early travel in Nigeria; in, for example, Lugard's account of the European traveller to whom the friendly chief of Shibi sent messages imploring him to await an escort before entering Borgu: 'The European pooh-poohed his friendly offers, with the result that the Borgu fell upon his caravan and dispersed and looted it, and the Frenchman himself was hit by a poisoned arrow and died.'[1]

The intuitive sympathy with which Cary first heard of the Maltby disaster caused him to heighten the verisimilitude of his tale by many details and episodes drawn from his own experience. The good-humoured relationship between Daventry and his carriers is that established between Cary and his own carriers when he trekked away from Lokoja in September 1916, with Maltby still very much in his thoughts. Many details recall the pleasure that he took in this solitary journey, after some weeks in the uncongenial mess at Lokoja: the caravan leaving headquarters, with an escort of drummers and the carriers' piper marking its passage through the corn-fields in the early morning sunlight; the first carriers up the

[1] H. G. Herman Hodge: *Gazetteer of Ilorin Province* (1929), p. 34.

escarpment of the plateau standing silhouetted against the skyline, like figures on a Greek vase; the camp at night where Daventry sits at his table under a baobab tree, with a glass at his elbow and a pile of writing paper in front of him; or the morning halts for breakfast:

> By the stream was a lawn of bright emerald grass shaded by half a dozen large cotton trees. The table was laid for breakfast with a clean cloth which made a white patch in the middle of the green, and Sammy sat in a mist of pale blue smoke beside the nearest tree, surrounded by open boxes. The carriers made groups in the speckled sunlight, as if for some pastoral play, and two or three dabbled their legs in the water beyond.

For the attack itself and the march back Cary drew on rather earlier memories, of Montenegro and the Cameroons. The most vivid of these is perhaps the account of how the party breaks camp before dawn and marches in relatively good spirits through the warm, protective darkness, only to experience an agoraphobic terror when the sudden daylight reveals their helplessness.

Daventry is, however, far from being a tissue of reminiscences, the kind of 'anecdote without meaning' that Cary held many of his first attempts at fiction to be. The book has a clear theme. It is about the betrayal of innocence. Daventry's Hausa nickname, which means 'King of the Youths' has been given him in irony by his followers, who have recognized in him the deep uncertainty which underlies the bravado of youth:

> A young man looks for trouble just as he buys curious literature, out of curiosity – not curiosity about other people, but solely about himself. He longs to know what he is made of. This is the chief reason why armies are recruited by volunteers in wartime, because of young men's curiosity. No one in his senses would enlist merely to kill, much less to be killed. So that Daventry when he cursed Berewa, was glad to be there, in a place worthy of curses.

Daventry's march into Weji is thus a self-exploration. Significantly, it is a journey without maps; he has no human guide on to whom he can shift responsibility. The Secretariat passes the responsibility for his safety to Crompton, and Crompton passes it to Daventry himself, but Daventry's attempt to pass it a stage further to Langa fails. Langa has urged an escort, but he does not refuse to move without one. His message to Daventry is simply that 'he says he obeys':

> On the tallest falls the chief load, and Daventry, who has been pleased to
> overtop all men for the first time in his life, now felt a pressure. He would
> have been glad to shift the smallest part of the burden. Perhaps he had
> asked Musa if he was afraid to go to Weji for no other reason, than to
> make him carry his childish share. Now a sentence that would have
> flattered him two days before, took on a more sinister appearance.

Daventry has to fall back on his own resources, and this guidance
from within is more treacherous than the young pagan chief who
leads them all into an ambush. Daventry's 'unconvoluted public
school intelligence' does not reach very far. What passes with him
for decision is often only a stock response drawn from childhood
and schoolday patterns of behaviour. A jotting on the manuscript
sums up the theme of *Daventry* by saying 'he is the result of an
education; he is the new boy again; he is too instinctive'. An education in chivalry has so conditioned Daventry that, a moment after
the attack, he gallops unarmed into the high corn after Audu, and
then retires from the scene with all the appearance of sang-froid:
'As he had ridden in upon a punctilio of honour, not to desert a
comrade, though the comrade was a fool, though no help at all
could be given him, so again he retired at a walk because of a
prejudice, inhabiting his poor skull stuffed with the chimaeras of
education, that it was honourable and dignified so to do – that he
owed it to good form'. A similar punctilio forces Daventry to
attend to every injury, poisoned or not poisoned, incurred by his
party, before he dresses his own poisoned wound. It is all a matter of
face: of maintaining the ideal of the good leader, the white protector, guardian, and friend of the natives committed to his care.
The Africans in the story have the reality-principle which is lacking
in Daventry's behaviour. When the carriers refuse to swim a river;
Daventry reproves Audu for hitting out at them and crosses first
himself as an example to the party. Audu sees his point; but beats the
carriers into the water the minute Daventry has passed out of sight
and earshot. 'No one better than the Hausa can give honest praise to
one course of action and pursue another, no one divides more

sharply the ideal and sentimental from the real and expedient.'
Musa, Audu, and Sammy do not see Daventry as their heroic
protector, but as a capricious foreigner whose whims have led them
to their death. On the return journey, Musa dies cursing Daventry;
Audu, before he falls dead from the saddle, rambles on about the
money that Crompton has extracted from the country and is now
keeping in the cash tank to enrich himself; and the cook, Sammy,
whom Daventry tends at the cost of delaying his own return to
Barewa, dies with the reproach: 'For Chris' sake, wa's de good!
What for you come here? You no fit to do nuffin.'

For this bitter story of innocence betrayed by what is false within
– its own idealism – Cary chose a traditional form, the form of
many early ballads and of Coleridge's great romantic ballad: the
contrast between a hopeful and picturesque departure, and a disillusioned return. The diary-like detail of Daventry's march into
Weji is essential to this scheme; after the attack, we know just how
much ground has to be traversed before he will be within reach of
help. Cary manages the turn in the story with considerable narrative
skill. The state of euphoria in which Daventry approaches the pagan
villages, marvelling that he is given special pay by the Government
to go on this prolonged picnic in beautiful country, quietens the
next day to a placid pride which causes him to linger behind his
caravan, 'not only to give himself the pleasure of this lonely ride,
for like other romantic people he enjoyed his own company, but
also to make a more effective entry into the new territory. He
imagined the whole village already expectant, perhaps even now
sitting by the roadside, man, woman and child, looking out for the
white man.' But the village is empty. Determined to cling to his
romantic illusion, and not to lose face, Daventry drives the party on
when the only rational course of action would be to turn back. The
emptiness of the next village symbolizes the vacuity which gives
rise to Daventry's action. He wanders from one deserted compound
to another, as he steps through the débris of his own thoughts.

He was, however, in pitiable confusion. . . . Thus he glanced at his duty,
and it looked like egotism, he tried to perceive honour, and it gibbered

at him. He sought for self-respect in his strength of purpose (especially in his firmness of the day before) and found that he had made a dangerous fool of himself. While his plane tabling appeared the stupidest, the most imbecile of stratagems, the last resort of a coward physically afraid to carry straight on with his enterprise, morally afraid either to face the consequences of going on or to admit failure and turn back.

This in-and-out movement of the book is suspended from time to time by a flash-back to the uncomprehending pride of Daventry's destined parents-in-law and by the correspondence between their daughter, Alice, and Daventry. Cary uses this device to make clear the kind of values Daventry has acquired and the unrealistic demands these values make of him. Because it nourishes his idea of himself as the peaceful penetrator, a letter from Alice, sent after Daventry by runner, finally decides him to turn down the offer of an escort. 'It is really you who are sending me on this expedition', he writes, with a truthfulness that is ominous to the reader. This theme of a character betrayed by the romantic expectations of those he leaves behind is handled afresh in another unpublished short novel called *Tottenham*, conceived (I think) a few years after *Daventry*. *Tottenham* is an almost unbearable story about an eight-year-old child whose parents refuse to acknowledge how unhappy he is at boarding school, because to do so would involve a loss of face, of parental pride. Unconsciously aware of their feelings, he stops protesting and returns to school, where he drinks a bottle of Lysol and dies. The sub-title of the book is *Victim of Love*.

In *Daventry*, the letters and the flash-backs to England give a chance for a change also in the tone of the story to a sharp irony. Daventry writes with delight of the friendliness of the young pagan chief who is to lead the party to their deaths; he has promised Daventry he shall see plenty of the young men of the tribe on his way out. And with a complacent mock-modesty, Daventry congratulates himself, 'the fool of the family', on his success: 'If I knew more perhaps I would not understand pagans so well.' The whole point of the tale is in fact that Daventry does not know enough, because his education has never encouraged him to think; and the flat, matter-of-fact style in which the greater part of it is written is Cary's deliberate choice for showing that Daventry's long agony puts him wise on a great many matters: 'he has not been betrayed before, but now he was able to perceive that there was nothing surprising in betrayal'.

Thus as early as 1919 Cary was able to give a clear, pointed meaning to his recollections and intuitions and to find the formal means, in characters, construction and style, which would make his theme fully explicit. Yet *Daventry* remains an immature work, and Cary's reputation would not be helped if it were published. The immaturity reveals itself in what Cary termed the approach, which in this case is almost entirely negative and destructive. It is of course true that Daventry learns by experience. He is able to spot that the Secretariat's transfer of responsibility to Crompton is the counterpart to his own wish to place some responsibility for the expedition's fate on the unfortunate small boy, Musa. The end (cancelled in the manuscript) also suggests that Daventry has acquired some wisdom in place of the chivalrous ideals that have been so little use to him. Ibrahim extracts a testimonial from the dying Daventry and rides away on his master's horse: 'Daventry was quite aware of the theft, and now hearing the rattle of hoofs, smiled to himself. His education was complete. He even remarked to himself, "I know as much as Sammy now." He was too wise to cherish a futile resentment just as he perceived his former stupidity of ambition. "I've learnt a lot," he murmured to himself.' But all he has in fact learnt is the fundamental injustice of life; and Cary tells us in the Preface of *Aissa Saved* that this represented the beginning, not the end, of his own attempts to make sense of the world. Cynicism, he was to show in his second published novel, is only an inverted idealism; and the weakness of *Daventry* is that Cary handles his story cynically. The universal values which should be a novelist's theme have here got overlaid and distorted by (to use his own words) 'private subjective elements, prejudices, misunderstandings, and very likely subconscious motives'.

To some degree this cynicism, about 1919, was a sign of the times.

The bland official comment on Maltby's expedition, that it was 'a plucky attempt to pursue the peaceful penetration policy without any show of force, which unfortunately cost him his life', jarred on Cary just in the way that conventional public condolences on the casualties of the 1914-18 War stuck in the craw of writers like Owen and Sassoon. But the mood was also a personal one. Cary was innately romantic, and the motives which took him to Africa were not so very different from those he probed in *Daventry*. He certainly passed, in the earlier part of his African service, through a phase of extreme cynicism which was the obverse of his idealism, and which is found in the scraps of La Rochefoucauld-like writing which survive from that time (he was reading La Rochefoucauld on the voyage out in 1916). A contemporary who fought with him in the Cameroons remembers him as full of courage and initiative, but 'extremely cynical'. He made the same impression on people on his first arrival in Kontagora Province. Indeed, Daventry, apprehensive and alone, is in part a self-portrait of Cary in his first months in Borgu, where the maps, both literal and figurative, bore little relationship to the terrain.

Later on, in Borgu, Cary outgrew these anxieties and discovered a creative freedom of action which was to supply the basis of the philosophy he evolved for himself in the nineteen-twenties, a philosophy which challenged the fundamental injustice of life. But because *Daventry*, though written in 1919, was connected with an earlier phase in Cary's African career, it reflects a state of mind from which he had to free himself to achieve anything as a novelist, just as he had had to free himself from it to administer with any success his ten thousand square miles of Nigeria.

3

Cary said of his second unpublished novel about Nigeria: 'It is still in being but no one, least of all myself, will ever get a clue to its massive ruins.' Yet the story itself is neither long nor complicated.

The manuscript is vast only because Cary repeatedly re-wrote its episodes in an effort to discover their full significance for himself. He recalled this struggle years later, in a broadcast talk he wrote in 1956:

> The vast work upstairs was unfinished for a special reason. I simply lost control of it. It was about a district officer in a remote part of Nigeria, among primitive pagans, usually alone, a dictator in a small way but also very fond of his people. I had been all these things myself and knew the life extremely well. I had got stacks of material and any amount of first-hand description. The man was called Jarvis; the book was to be called *Cock Jarvis*.

('Unfinished Novels')

The story of *Cock Jarvis* remains fairly constant through all Cary's re-writings. Jarvis is Resident of Daji, which he conquered in the nineties. He rules it like an independent prince, until he gets into trouble with the central government for turning a blind eye to the misdeeds of the Emir. As a result, the Province is reduced to a division. At this or an earlier date, Jarvis has married. The situation in which he meets his future wife varies from version to version, but his motives for marrying a woman much younger than himself are always chivalrous and protective; in Cary's phrase, he is romantic all through. He recommends for appointment to the Political Service a young man called (usually) Thompson, without realizing he is his wife's former lover. Thompson is put in charge of Shibi, a sub-district of Daji. His criticism of Jarvis's administration precipitates a new crisis and a commission of enquiry. Jarvis's wife has asked her husband for a divorce, and leaves to return to England; the company of troops is withdrawn from the station, and Jarvis is left alone. He discovers that his wife has in fact gone off with Thompson. The story ends with Jarvis's suicide; in some outlines he pursues and shoots Thompson before taking his own life.

As Cary said, he had stacks of material for this story. Thompson's life in the sub-district is closely modelled on Cary's in Borgu; he builds zungos and bridges, campaigns against guinea-worm, and tries to disentangle intricate complaints. The incident which occasions the second inquiry is particularly authentic: Thompson comes to Daji to complain that Moma, a protégé of the Emir, has abducted a young girl from Shibi. As Jarvis refuses to arrest Moma, he does so himself; Moma escapes and the girl is found bayoneted. Other scenes and incidents remembered by Cary from his West Coast days are connected with Jarvis: the disembarkment of deck passengers on to lighters outside the Accra surf, carried out with a real West African disregard for life and limb until the paternalistic Jarvis thunders to the sailors and officials that they are to look after 'his people'; the desolation of a bush station planned as the nucleus of a future city and then abandoned – a memory of Zungeru; and Jarvis's triumphal return to his province with his young bride:

> The Niger was then Jarvis's boundary, and he was received on the further shore by the chiefs of Shibi, Kaza, by Momar Maidoli, representing the Emir of Daji, and by several hundred village chiefs, petitioners, farmers, etc., of whom a great number joined his camp and travelled south with him towards Daji town. Jarvis's camp was notorious throughout the country for disorder and noise, so that even devoted junior officers tried to excuse themselves from travelling with him. Wherever he went in his own country he was surrounded by a mob of hangers-on, litigants, beggars, tradesmen, parasites and their parasites, cranks, prostitutes, thieves, ambitious people, musicians, poets and learned men, maniacs, whom he refused to drive away because he considered it his duty to be in touch with the people.
>
> Kate was disgusted by the sights and smells, the lack of privacy, the impossibility of sleeping which made this march horrible to her, but when she asked Jarvis to drive away some of the more noisy drunkards, and some of those infected by diseases of which the idea made her ill he answered with surprise that he could not do so.
>
> 'Poor devils,' he said. 'They come to me to do what I can for them. They consider themselves my people, and so they are.'
>
> 'But they might stay a little further off.'
>
> 'I don't like to hurt their feelings,' and twirling his moustache he said gravely 'You see – I'm a kind of king here – and noblesse oblige.'
>
> 'Yes – I can see you spoil them like everybody else.'
>
> But he was disappointed that Kate did not enjoy the excitement, power and glories of her position as his royal consort. . . .

The seed of *Cock Jarvis* in Cary's mind was not, however, any of these personal experiences, vivid as the memory of them was, but the story he had heard in 1914 when he first went to Bauchi of how a Resident of that province had committed suicide there in 1908. That is to say *Cock Jarvis* started as a story of defeat, like *Daventry* and *Tottenham*. But if Cary began the tale with the intention that it should show a good man destroyed through ingratitude, injustice and betrayal, he grew dissatisfied with his theme as he wrote, and perhaps because of what he wrote. The chief interest of the *Cock Jarvis* manuscript is that we can discover in it the embryonic forms of themes which Cary was to develop successfully in his published novels, but could not handle in this abandoned one because its original impetus was in a contrary direction.

Thus when Cary looked back at *Cock Jarvis* in 1956, he saw that it might have taken shape as a political novel:

> [Jarvis] believed in the Empire, in fact, as the only hope of liberal civiliza-
> tion in the world, and he would say that the fall of the Roman Empire
> before the tribes of nationalist barbarians had wrecked civilization for a
> thousand years. And would do it again if they could smash the British
> Empire.
>
> My problem was to show that though Jarvis was right in principle he
> was wrong in fact because the Empire couldn't last – it was up against
> powers that would certainly destroy it and the problem was therefore to
> dissolve or transform it in such a way that it wouldn't be succeeded by a
> thousand years of barbarians, war and misery. What I had on my hands
> was a study of an honest man who didn't understand what politics was
> about. But I couldn't manage my material or my characters.
>
> ('Unfinished Novels')

But this was a long view, in the light of the mid-century's clarifica-tion of colonial issues. When he actually wrote *Cock Jarvis*, Cary was not able to distinguish between the old protective liberalism which inspired the philosophy of indirect rule and the new liberalism of aid and development which was still powerless to be born. He was guided at the time more by his sympathies than by any objective understanding of the situation; and his sympathies were all with the giants before the flood, with the original Residents of Nigeria who were, he felt, misunderstood by the new-style administrators who went out in numbers after the First World War. Not that he drew any direct portrait in *Cock Jarvis*. Drafting a letter to his publisher in 1935, he insisted: 'I take very great trouble to avoid identification of any described character, even a good one, with a real person. This is a considerable sacrifice, as you would understand, if you had known some of my old colleagues in the service, either political or military, o n the old coast' (N85). Certainly none of the men Cary admired in Nigeria could have treated the Secretariat quite so cavalierly as Cock Jarvis. Yet personal affection colours such a piece of writing as Jarvis's letter to Thompson congratulating him on increasing trade in his district. It is a characteristically magnanimous letter, since Jarvis has earlier quarrelled with Thompson about roads which will, he fears, bring everything he hates under the name of progress:

> I see you have spent a hundred and fifty pounds on roads in the last three months. The whole sum allowed by the Treasury for Shibi roads is twenty pounds, so be careful to make out vouchers for that amount, and charge ten to special messengers, five to stationery, five to extra assistance in the office and three pounds three and fourpence to capital works, whatever you like, say repairs to courthouse roof. Of the other ninety pounds odd, I can raise thirty on Daji votes and the rest I shall collar out of this year's taxes. The Emir and I can trust each other and that proves to be a blessing for Shibi as well as Daji. I need not tell you this arrangement is not to be published in 'Advice to the A.D.O.s by one of them.' It is strictly private, for the sake of the Treasurer, who would go off in a fit at the very idea.
>
> But you've been rather extravagant lately; I don't mind your spending three times as much as you've got in the bank, but anything over and above five times might appear to a base barnacle or member of council like an invitation to display the badness of his manners and the narrowness of his mind.

Cary's repeated rewritings of this kind of episode show that he realized that personal experience was getting in the way of the story as he planned it. This kind of easy and affectionate relationship between the two men in the story would not do if it had to end with Thompson hounding Jarvis to death. But his attempts to objectify the relationship only resulted in Thompson becoming unpleasant past the bounds of probability; Jarvis, that is to say, could not be 'placed' or 'distanced' in any way, because Cary could not detach himself from him. Thus rewriting only made the story more a tale of defeat than before, and could not transform it to a dramatic struggle between the political ideals of two generations.

The rivalry of Jarvis and Thompson for Jarvis's wife – variously called Kate or Nancy – also prevented *Cock Jarvis* from becoming a successful political novel. It is conceivable that Cary might, in time, have got his chief character sufficiently into perspective for the reader not to feel his political ruin as a tragic event; but this was impossible as long as the sex-triangle of the plot threw all the reader's sympathy back on to Jarvis. Cary himself admits in his notes that the political story did not dovetail well with the love interest. When he does try to connect them, the reader always finds he is identifying himself with Jarvis. This happens when Kate and her friends amuse themselves at Jarvis's expense: 'In appearance, and in the way he strutted, curled his moustache with three fingers, and in his dandified dress, and in his politics, he was exactly like the comic soldier on the stage, very downright, rather hot-tempered and perfectly feudal in his ideas.' Once our sympathies have been directed like this, the story becomes a wholly pathetic tale of a good man defeated and outwitted by two callow people. The proposal to make Jarvis shoot Thompson (a scene never actually written) represents a half-conscious attempt on Cary's part to deliver Jarvis from this doom of pity. In an unjust world, the man of honour attempts to make his own justice. But at the time he wrote *Cock Jarvis* this way of making his hero avert defeat was not yet clear to him.

Cary tried one other way of making Jarvis resist the world's fundamental injustice. This was to give his hero a strengthening faith. He made, however, a bad start in this development, to judge by a fairly early section inscribed 'Cocky finding Jesus'. Jarvis, when he rides out with the doctor and the Army officers on their final departure from the station, declares he does not need any sympathy for the seeming failure of his career: 'I'm happier now than ever I was in my life before, because I've gone down to bedrock. I have my feet on Christ and nothing can touch me now.' This rings painfully false; and the reason is that while Cary was becoming increasingly convinced at this time that religious certainty was the most valid response to injustice, he was dissatisfied with any faith that offered security and repose. Jarvis sheltered by the Rock of Ages is not a convincing figure; nor is Jarvis quoting 'he that seeks his life shall lose it'. Quietism and otherworldliness were both evasions of life's perpetual battle, to Cary's way of thinking. And there are signs in other parts of the manuscript that this way of thinking was developing fast as Cary wrote the novel. Occasionally Jarvis appears in a much more convincing guise as a militant Christian, claiming to 'hit them over the head with the Sermon on the Mount', riding the waves of injustice with something of Gulley Jimson's energy. But his determination not to hate, to remain generous and to go on to the next thing, only makes his final defeat the more improbable and so the novel itself more difficult to finish.

It was in fact impossible for Cary to complete the novel without entirely changing the ending. The three years he spent writing *Cock Jarvis* were years in which he was evolving a personal philosophy which could challenge the bad luck of existence. For this reason, he could not be satisfied with a hero who gave up the struggle. At the same time, he was too near to the phase of cynicism in which he wrote *Daventry* to detach himself entirely from his hero's experience of life's injustice. Cary, that is to say, never succeeded in clarifying his own relationship to Jarvis, and consequently never found a satisfactory form for his book. The three chief characters change their natures completely from one draft to the next, running, as they do so, through as many personalities as there are possible angles in a triangle. And the style of the book lacks the firmness of *Daventry*, in which Cary had been confident of his approach and as yet unaware of its inadequacies.

But Cary was unwilling to let Cock Jarvis fade away. Some of his traits reappear in Bewsher of *An American Visitor*. Again, in *Castle Corner* Cary made use of the division of interest between Britain and Africa to separate the political interest of *Cock Jarvis* from the marriage story, and to use only the first in the African sections of the novel. Jarvis's conquest of Daji was to be only the prelude to his

African adventures in two or three sequels. But *Castle Corner* had a mediocre press, and Cary abandoned the idea of a family saga divided between England, Ireland and Nigeria. Jarvis, however, still stuck in his imagination; at one time after the trilogy had been abandoned, he sketched out a plan for turning the original tale into a long-short story in which Jarvis in his deserted bush station was to be a typical Cary character. Here called Ballsard, he is an ageing District Officer 'exiled to a mudheap, who sets out to make a life of it – makes a garden, asks the mish to dinner. His idea of the right thing – full of energy and pride. Four silver candles on table.' His daughter 'tells him not an autocrat any more, but a failure, ought to retire for health's sake. She worried about consequences but no effect at all. She doesn't understand that he is not really deceiving himself or acting a part but *creating* experience for himself from day to day' (N62). About the same time as this was written Cary sketched out yet one more scheme for *Cock Jarvis* in which 'Point of Cocky is that his *work* is destroyed – his preservation work – and he shoots the man who does it, quite sincerely'. Here Cary is concerned with a type of character less congenial to him than 'Ballsard': the man who takes up arms against a sea of troubles instead of riding the surf. Both, however, represent a positive response to the world's incalculable bad luck, whereas the suicide of the original Cock Jarvis was no answer at all.

In his second, political trilogy of novels, published in the nineteen-fifties, Cary brought together these last two developments of the original Cock Jarvis in the person of Jim Latter. The fact that Latter figures in two of the three novels gave Cary the opportunity he needed to separate the marriage theme and the African theme, which combined so uneasily in the earlier manuscript, as well as the chance to develop separately the Latter who rises buoyantly above his luck and the Latter who makes his own justice. In *Not Honour More*, Latter kills his wife because he has to clear away the fog of deceit and treachery enveloping three lives. This represents to some degree a creative response to the world's injustice. Yet Latter is not really free in his actions. As Cary had noted down of Cock Jarvis some years earlier, when he was still planning continuations to *Castle Corner*, Latter is 'captive of a sense of justice'. The really free man is the younger Latter of *Prisoner of Grace*, which critics have found much the better novel. After devoting the best years of his life to the Luga tribe, Latter finds himself written off by the British public and by the Lugas themselves as a reactionary, whose wish to keep the tribe from the more doubtful benefits of civilization is interpreted as racial discrimination and the worst sort of imperialism. But the Latter of this book does not shoot anyone. Like Cock Jarvis left alone in the deserted Daji station, he goes on to the next thing, which is a garden: 'It was quite time he got down to something he understood, like growing cabbages.'

The real trouble with *Cock Jarvis*, Cary said in the broadcast already quoted, was that 'it was far too ambitious. It took on too big a subject. It went on raising fundamental questions about religion and politics, to which, to my naïve surprise, I found I hadn't got the answer.' Cary however exaggerated in saying he wasted three years over *Cock Jarvis*. The work was a huge mistake, but a profitable one. Cary needed a wealth of written material, such as the manuscript provided, to help him discover the thin places in his own view of life. But this discovery took longer than three years. 'I had to re-educate myself as a novelist, and it took me more than ten years. Nothing I wrote during nine of those years was published – it was mostly unfinished, and what I finished I didn't like. I grew out of my books as fast as I wrote them. My first published novel, *Aissa Saved*, which looks so simple a job, took three years to do, and is full of technical mistakes. But it was the first that didn't raise questions I couldn't answer, and didn't dodge them' ('My First Novel').

Was Aissa Saved?

I

When Joyce Cary's first novel, *Aissa Saved*, appeared in 1932, the reviewers were impressed but disconcerted. For one thing, the book turned their stomachs. Most of them based their reviews on this reaction, defining Cary's theme as the savagery of primitive religion, and protesting at his absolutely objective descriptions of the rites of human sacrifice. And the form of the book occasioned as much critical discomfort as its theme and tone; the *Spectator*'s reviewer spoke for all when he complained that Cary had failed to stage-manage his mob of unruly characters.

Aissa Saved is certainly what Henry James would call a crammed book – so crammed that the reader may well feel that the author loses sight of his main story in the hurly-burly of events. The main tale itself is simple in outline: Aissa, the favourite convert of Mr and Mrs Carr, missionaries on the Niger, leads her fellow-Christians in a holy war against the juju of the pagans across the river; in the course of this, young Ali, the educated Moslem protégé of the District Officer, Bradgate, is butchered by a Christian mob, and Aissa finally sacrifices her own child in a rain-making ceremony designed to prove the superiority of the Christian faith. But to give dramatic form to this story, Cary employs, in barely two hundred pages, upwards of seventy named characters. As all but four of them are African, it is not surprising that he quickly ran out of names in writing the book. When he had exhausted his recollections of court cases and tax assessments in Borgu – the setting of the novel according to one manuscript version, which locates Shibi north of the Bussa rapids – he had to supplement his memory by recourse to anthropological works on Southern Nigeria. For a Nigerian reader the result resembles a novel set in Stoke-on-Trent in which the characters are called Leonardo and Ivanovitch.

It is, however, important to realize at the outset that Cary did not at any time write a novel 'about' Nigeria. In *Aissa Saved* he used Borgu and Kontagora as a satisfyingly distanced setting for a book about the fundamental injustice of the world and the varying faiths by which individuals come to their own terms with this injustice. Cary's preface to the Carfax edition makes plain that this, rather than the parallel savageries of juju and debased Christianity, is the theme of the book; and we shall see that its tone, far from having the objectivity complained of by reviewers, errs on the side of too great an involvement. As for Cary's conduct of the story, once we have seized the book's theme we are likely to complain that it has too much form rather than too little. It is a sinewy book, in which not only each episode, but every sentence illustrates the theme of the individual's response to life's injustice. Our discomfort in reading it comes less from any horrors of the story than from the unrelenting thematic use to which much of the story is put. The sensation is that of looking in a mirror and seeing only bone and muscle, the anatomy of life, whereas the experience we seek is rather that defined by Cary in his praise of Conrad: 'life recognizing itself'.

The fundamental injustice of the world took well-defined forms for Joyce Cary. First, there was the permanent character of being itself, the world which science examines, the world of genes and chromosomes, whose misadventures bring about the defects of birth. But there were other accidents of birth besides the physical; time and place might be out of joint for a particular individual. And sometimes the injustice of the world might take the form, not of physical fact or social situation, but of the hurt derived from an inevitable clash of wills in the closed ring of marriage or family life. So in *Aissa Saved* the permanent nature of the world is represented by the long drought which brings hunger to Yanrin; the injustice of society shows itself in the cruelty of the pagans to the Christian Aissa or of an illiterate community to the educated Ali; and everywhere in the book there is fierce hand-to-hand fighting between incompatible personal views of life. It has to be a violent tale because Cary is concerned with the individual's reaction to the violence of bad luck. 'The question is, how sound is the faith; how will it stand the big knock; how deep does it send its roots into reality' (Carfax preface, p. 8).

There are people who can accept injustice as the inevitable condition of the created world and then, absorbed in their own act of creation, in making their own lives, they forget or discard it. Such people, to quote a letter from Cary to Mark Schorer, include 'Mister Johnson, who simply forgets his grievance, who lives in creation, Gulley Jimson who is aware of the dilemma and knows that he must not hate the injustice of the world, that he too must live in creation'. Johnson is a boy, Gulley an old man; to be able to discard injustice requires youth or the wisdom of age. The youngest character in *Aissa Saved*, Aissa's baby, Abba, is knocked down in his parents' horse-play, and at first resents their blandishments:

> She rocked it in her arms and offered it her breast. But it, slighted by this bribe instead of the reparation justly demanded by its injuries, sunk its head between its shoulders like a tortoise, curled its back, stiffened its arms, pulled down the corners of its mouth, and uttered a loud howl.
>
> This made Aissa as well as Gajere shout with laughter. . . . Aissa tossed it up and shouted, 'There we go.' These insults caused Abba to howl with rage. He knew very well that he was not going to get any compensation for his injustice, he was being cheated. But suddenly he forgot this huge grievance and smiled.
>
> (p. 198)

Adult resentment cannot be so quickly forgotten; but it can be discarded in the business of getting on with the job. To get on with the job in the teeth of the world's injustice requires faith in the job, and in oneself as well: the Conradian virtues of self-respect and self-reliance, of a proper pride. In *Aissa Saved*, Ali, the young Assistant Treasurer who has learnt at the school for chiefs' sons not only to write Hausa in Roman characters, but also to rely on himself and take responsibility, can discard the misunderstanding and even the brutal ill-treatment of the decadent palace community to whom he, as the son of a slave, appears a braggart upstart. 'But though people thought nothing of Ali, it appeared now that he thought a good deal of himself' (p. 88). 'Whence did the son of a slave, not sixteen years old, ugly, friendless, poor, derive such reckless self-confidence, such rash energy?' (p. 95). When *The Times Literary Supplement*, in an inept review, accepted the palace evaluation of Ali and called him 'a typical swelled-head', Cary was moved to write one of his very rare letters of self-defence. Perhaps it was not so much a self-defence as championship of the original of Ali, the young court scribe who had assisted Cary in his last months in Borgu and for whom he had felt real affection, as his official papers show. The relationship is reflected in the novel, where Bradgate's praise delights the boy because 'his words had told Ali what, like other boys newly put into the world, he most wanted to know and had the most difficulty in finding out, what he was worth. They assured him that he was a person of value, a somebody, and he was intoxicated with relief and pride' (p. 119).

Such proud self-assertion seemed to Cary a much better response to the world's wrongs than any form of self-abdication. 'Unselfishness', he wrote in his Borgu diary, 'is by the nature of things a possession. Where self is not, something else which is not self, must be. Some unselfish people are possessed by good spirits, some by bad.' The word *possession* indicates a religious experience; and in the novel the ethical code of Bradgate and of the Government school at Berua (where Ali has presumably received that 'moral instruction' dear to the heart of Lugard) is opposed by the religious abandon of Christians and pagans alike. Their enthusiasm (in the eighteenth-century sense) is illustrated by the experiences undergone by Aissa on her return to the mission after her capture and ill-treatment by the pagans of Kolu. Aissa, who is by nature as splendidly resilient as Ali, has fought a long and terrible struggle for self-preservation in the hope of finding her lover and baby safe at the mission. Now, her fellow-converts, after consulting the biblical 'oracle', assure her that Abba and Gajere are not only dead but in Hell. Aissa despairs. 'Aissa knew that she had a bad spirit in her but she did not care. She did not want to drive it out. She liked it because it gave her pain and

told her to be angry' (p. 136). In the full meaning of the phrase, she
lets herself go, and becomes that mysterious figure described by
every European missionary and school-teacher, the African who lies
down to die. When she is found by Mrs Carr she seems to be dead
'because she has done with life and everything and everybody in it'
(p. 147). Mrs Carr's consolations do not reach her; relief comes
below the rational level, in the singing of the mission's converts who
crowd round her, crooning the hymn, 'I am not worthy, Lord':

> The rhythm played on Aissa, it poured through her body in waves; it
> went through the bad spirit making him soft and weak, it washed him
> away like sand.
>
> (pp. 148-9)

Demonic possession is succeeded by divine possession at Aissa's
first communion:

> What would Jesus do inside her? What would he feel like? What would
> he say? She perceived a faint warmth in her stomach. She brought all her
> mind upon the place. She held her breath. But the feeling had gone
> already. Where was it? She found it again deeper and further in. It grew
> quickly, it was like the morning sun whose rays grow stronger and
> warmer every minute; it pierced through the cold muscles; it passed
> outwards through the whole body in waves of heat burning out all her
> cold wickedness. It was making her like Jesus himself, pure so that she
> did not want Gajere any more, brave so that she was not afraid of the
> pagans, loving so that she loved Jesus with all her heart, happy so that she
> had never been so happy.
>
> (pp. 153-4)

Cary deliberately makes this account orgastic: the experience itself is
not religious, though it can be given a religious application. Its
sequence of self-abandonment, possession by evil spirits, exorcism
of the evil spirits and possession by a good spirit, has found
expression in many religions and, Cary believed, has distorted the
best of them. It has perverted Christianity to a religion of blood-
sacrifice whose adherents, attributing the injustice of the world to
their own sins, seek a scapegoat whose sufferings will free them from
all responsibility. Some such idea of the atonement informs the
extraordinary sermon preached by the mission's star pupil, Ojo, in

the middle of the festival of Oke at Kolu. But Ojo is preaching to
the converted; the Kolua have already decided that the prolonged
drought is a visitation for their sins and have prepared a human
sacrifice to appease the righteous anger of their goddess.

2

Once we have grasped Cary's distinction between self-reliance and
self-abandonment as two forms of response to the world's injustice,
almost every character and incident in *Aissa Saved* (we shall find
significant exceptions) is seen to demonstrate one of these responses.

The District Officer, Bradgate, is a man who takes sensibly short
views and is well versed in the art of the possible. 'Bradgate was a
good political officer, that is to say, he never forgot his job was
politic – to make the best of given circumstances, whatever they
were' (p. 82). Accepting the world as he finds it, he tells the Kolua
that the famine is due to a slump and bad weather, which cannot be
helped; and takes advantage of the prolonged dry season to build
bridges which will bring trade to Yanrin, and so lessen the chances
of famine returning. Bradgate's bridge-building exploits are exactly
modelled on those of Joyce Cary himself in the days when he had
been D.O., Borgu. In his attempt to build a bridge near Bussa in the
early months of 1919, Cary had to endure all Bradgate's frustrations.
As he wrote to his wife:

> I had asked them to collect bridge material, and mend the house, – the
> bridge to be done first. They did nothing to the bridge – but they have
> taken half the roof off the house. This was a pleasant surprise for a tired
> homecomer. My voice was not much louder than a bronchitic grass-
> hopper's as I explained to them the house was done untimely – and the
> bridge would now never be done at all.

> (22 February 1919)

Cary went back to his headquarters at Kaiama (building a successful
bridge on the way). When he returned to the neighbourhood of
Bussa a month later, he wrote to his wife:

As I advance up the country a wave of industry proceeds before me. I hear the Emir of Bussa is frantically building the bridge which should have been finished a month ago – he started the day before yesterday. The work at the Woko bridge had only just been accomplished when I arrived. What a glorious time they would all have if we all went away – I mean the chiefs.

(13 March 1919)

Cary was then drawn away, like Bradgate, on a boundary commission, and returned to find

them making a botch of it. I was annoyed, but it is no good being annoyed. These people are as God made 'em, and nothing can teach 'em to take any pride in a job of work – not at any rate the chiefs. . . . The Emir, knowing this bridge was to be built and being within 12 miles of the bridge I wanted him to copy – was too slack to go and look at it. He sent a servant.

(28 March 1919)

I quote these passages from Cary's letters because they help to fix for us his attitude towards Bradgate. Most of the satire is directed, not at Bradgate himself, but at the social system within which Bradgate struggles to get on with the job; at the base barnacles (Cary's expression) of Kaduna who, engaged in a private war between the Treasury and the P.W.D., don't allow him any money to do the job, and at the governmental policy which backs the Emirs. A vivid but spiteful vignette of indirect rule is afforded by the scene in which Bradgate flounders enthusiastically in the mud of the river bed, while on its bank the Emir and his court are deploring the incursion of Yorubas which the bridge will bring, and the senior pagan member of the Council is quietly planning to burn it down at the first opportunity. But neither the injustice of the heavens nor the obtuseness of pagans, Christians, Moslems and bureaucrats can overcome Bradgate's resilience; his job is to build bridges. And ranked on Bradgate's side are members of every social group who, whatever God they trust in, are careful to keep their powder dry.

The sense of responsibility, of being entrusted with a job to do, is particularly strong among the pagan children. In his Borgu diary, Cary had pondered the question of whether or not a universal moral sense operated in societies whose moral codes were different from those of Western Europe, and decided the common factor was the sense of duty. It is this sense which carries the small girl, Tanawe, who is sent to Bradgate with news of the first Kolu riot, through wild crowds, and along a ghost-ridden bush track:

> For one thing she had to do what she was told, and for another she would have been ashamed to fail in an important grown-up task. Tanawe had been trained to consider virtue those qualities which being equally valuable to parents and admired by the world that also profits by them are virtue everywhere. She had learnt to be dutiful and to serve a common purpose. She knew that it was shameful to fail in one's duty, to be a coward, to be mean or selfish, and this knowledge enforced by example and teaching and many slaps, had reached every part of her body so that her legs were now conducting themselves with great bravery while her mind was not so brave.
>
> (pp. 65-6)

Exactly the same eagerness of children and adolescents to know what they ought to do and to fit themselves into the scheme of things is shown by the small boy who runs for a pestle when the witch's limbs are to be broken, the youth who helps kidnap the pagan mother, Ishe, so that she may assist at the sacrifice of her son to the goddess, and the young boy who gives away Ali to the mob of demented Christians. Words like 'duty' and 'responsibility', which occur again and again in Cary's account of such incidents, are used not with irony, but as serious praise for those who, according to their lights, do their job well.

There is praise also for Musa, the headman of Kolu town, whose violent irruption into any quarrel 'uttering cries of indignation which sounded like a duck quacking' is comical to strangers, but not to the natives of the town, who respect his honesty and courage. Musa meets the injustice of the world in the person of the Carrs, who, resenting his attempts to keep order at their prayer-meeting, humiliate him before the whole town by telling him sharply to go away. But he hasn't time for resentment; fresh calls on his services send him off uttering curses and threats, and in the end he saves the lives of the reluctant Carrs by getting them off to their boats. Zeggi, the Yanrin chief of police, is a similar character. He is a veteran of many wars, who

> had grasped the notions of duty and obedience, of routine and even the idea of them. He knew why they were valuable, and like other simple men who have acquired by chance or instruction some fragment of systematic knowledge, he set the highest value on it. It was his religion, his touchstone, his glory.
>
> (p. 102)

With a full sense of his responsibility, Zeggi sets about curing the witch, Aissa, who has been consigned to the prison at Yanrin. Ignoring the jeers of the irresponsible, he gets the best medical advice available – a *mallam* and a Yoruba trader – and thanks to their care and his own skilful amputation of Aissa's gangrened foot, he restores her to health. But instead of the praise he hoped to receive from Bradgate he gets an order from the Native Authority – the local council of four pagans and four Moslems – to get rid of the woman at once. Again there is no satirical intention in the account of how Zeggi applies himself to this new task. Cary has nothing but admiration for a man who can brush off injustice without a grudge. The satire is all directed at the absurdities of the political system which wasted the talents of Nigeria's many Zeggis by expecting them to serve two masters at once.

Cary finds it less easy to be fair with the Southern immigrants into this Northern Emirate. He never quite rid himself of the ancient prejudice of the British administrators against the lawyers, traders, and clerks of the Coast. But those among them who act according to their lights get their due: even the villainous cook Jacob, who 'had a great respect for himself, but it was founded on a reasonable basis for he practised all the virtues and possessed all the accomplishments which were most admired by the lower ranks of [European] trader among whom he had been bred' (pp. 78-9). A better Southern environment has produced Clerk Williams, who is modelled, as we know from *The Case for African Freedom*, upon the clerk, Mr Graves, in Borgu, whose sense of duty once caused him to check a fight single-handed. The Moslems too have their responsibilities: as the father of his people, the Emir is distressed that he is unable to relieve the penury of his old friend and fellow-warrior, Haji Sali, who is seventy-five and very infirm; he leaps at the opportunity of proposing him to Bradgate as Minister of Bridges. Waziri too (the Vizier) must fulfil his responsibility, which for an emancipated slave means first and foremost he must provide for his family; to do this he has to keep on the right side of the Emir by beating all the subversive Western nonsense out of his European-educated son, Ali. For him the world's injustice takes the form of Bradgate's refusal, after a very good dinner at the mission, to listen to any complaints against the Christians. 'For a long time his voice could be heard as he retreated slowly towards the town, lamenting to the stars and to Allah the difficulties of a waziri and the follies of judges' (p. 142).

But Waziri is a tenacious old man, who continues to fight for his own place in the scheme of things. He belongs with the self-reliant and not the self-surrendering, with those who resist and not with those who evade the injustice of life. The position of his master, the Emir, is more ambiguous. Though his concept of himself as the father of his people may stir him into action on behalf of Haji Sali, he has a very scanty understanding of the duties of a ruler over a mixed population; when the Christians carry their holy war into Yanrin, he and his courtiers fold their hands and do nothing. They do not, of course, want to do anything which may upset the mysterious British. But the focus of the satire here shifts from the anomalies of indirect rule to the mentality of the courtiers who prefer youth in Paradise to old age in Yanrin. In fact Islam, to Cary's way of thinking, bred both the affirmation and the abnegation of self: he admired the self-reliance which refused all mediation between God and man, but deplored the fatalism which abandoned action in face of the will of Allah, and looked to an after-life to compensate for the injustice of the present.

3

Among the pagans and Christians in *Aissa Saved*, as among the Moslems, there are many who are ready to surrender their self-possession for possession by god or devil. The sequence of religious possession is experienced by various inmates of the mission who want to be compensated for the way nature and society have treated them. They include not only Nangulo, highway robber and murderer, and the crazed epileptic, Shangoedi, but also Mrs Carr, who has lost her first child as Aissa appears to have done: 'She needed often to remind herself of her happiness and comfort in the love of Jesus' (p. 148). Among the pagans, too, resentment at wrongs from which there is no redress projects itself into religious experience. The goddess Oke 'showed herself to an epileptic girl at twilight on the Yanrin road, and bitterly complained of the people's bad conduct towards her' (p. 31). Even the healthiest have a grudge which must be worked off in the ritual dance which precedes the sacrifice to Oke:

> Not only the debtors, beggars, prostitutes, lepers, diseased wretches, ruptured children, syphilitic girls, idiots and outcasts, but those who seemed strong and well and to have no cares, leapt and grimaced with fierce, greedy cries and wild gestures which seemed to throw off heavy burdens of fear and anxiety; which said: 'I don't care for anybody, I don't care for anything. I'll do what I like this time.'
>
> Only the old men and women with bodies twisted by work and disease, their grey faces hollow like rain-eaten stones, continued to look on, or pretending to join in, shuffled with bored patient looks, like those who perform a duty without much hope of profit.
>
> (p. 54)

On a superficial reading, little difference may be noticed between these ironic accounts of the self-abandoned and those which we have already glanced at of the self-possessed; between, say, Cary's account of the pagan priest's son fending off the attack on his father's shrine and then, 'feeling his responsibility discharged', crawling back disembowelled to die; and his allusion to the young Kolua girl 'intelligent and warmhearted beyond her years', who 'cut herself so badly in devotion to the goddess that she died' (p. 125). Only when such passages are viewed in relation to the whole story are Cary's praises of the self-reliant found to be serious admiration and his praises of the self-abandoned to be wholly damning. 'Self-sacrifice', he writes in a notebook, 'as an ideal (for its own sake) is moral defeatism or sensual indulgence. It is probably pathological either in origin or manifestation, and belongs to all primitive religion' (N39). A key passage indicative of this is the 'conversion' of the missionary Carr, which occurs early in the novel.

The more enthusiastic converts of the mission want to go to preach the gospel in the pagan town of Kolu at the time of the Oke festival. Carr, from a sense of responsibility, objects; but in the night Aissa and Ojo and their fellow Christians make for the boats and Mrs Carr, believing in Ojo's 'call', goes with them. Carr sets off in pursuit and in so doing literally stubs his toes on the hard, unjust facts of the physical world:

> But he was in such a hurry and fright that he lost his way, tumbled into holes and thickets and did not see the smoke and flames blowing from the lantern which peppered him with large black smuts. Finally, it went out, and left him struggling in a thicket. He did not reach Shibi by the short-cut, a mile long, in half an hour.
>
> (p. 21)

As the result of these mishaps, he finds the whole party, including his wife, already embarking. He has to go with them, in a mood of bitter resentment at the world's unfairness:

> And why had the lamp failed him? It had plenty of oil in it. It had never played tricks before. But why should he be surprised, luck was always against him – if one could call an enemy so persistent and malignant, luck.
>
> (p. 25)

The temptation to let go is strong: 'Was he not the biggest fool of the whole party to throw away his health and peace of mind and his best years on such a struggle?' At this point, just as the day breaks with sudden, tropical brilliance, the boats are caught in a strong eddy and Carr's canoe is carried after the others as if it were flying downhill. Things are beyond Carr's control, and he in fact suddenly lets go, abandoning himself to the beauty of the morning, to the voices of the converts as their song is carried over the water, and above all to his wife's religious ardour.

> He saw, as in a flash of lightning, the way out of the dark confusion in which he had been struggling so long and desperately, with problems never to be finally solved and difficulties renewed every day, the way of faith which he had been pointing out to savages daily for ten years and wandered from himself.

> 'Trust God,' he had told them; 'take no thought for the morrow,' while he had been trusting everything and everybody but God, his own intelligence and forethought most of all.

The party is singing his favourite hymn: 'None of self and all of Thee':

> None of self and all of thee – there was no middle way. All his hours of anxious planning, his nights of apprehension made unnecessary. Brain and nerves and courage enjoyed release like a resurrection. He did not care for anything or anyone.

(pp. 28-9)

As the point of view adopted here is that of Carr himself, Cary's own moral placing of his conversion as a disastrous surrender has to be conveyed to us in the book's subsequent events: in the echo of the phrase, 'did not care for anything or anyone'; in accounts of the pagan worshippers and of Aissa's conversion which I have already quoted; in the praise of a character like Ali, which makes plain Cary's belief that no one has any right to relinquish intelligence and forethought or to cease to use brain, nerves, and courage; in the riots and warfare which follow the expedition to Kolu and undo the patient political work of years.

A striking feature of this final holocaust is that all its atrocities are performed by women. Shangoedi and Aditutu catch Musa by a ruse and cut his throat; Zeggi is hacked to pieces by women in the Christians' attack on the palace at Yanrin; Ali is tortured to death by the demented Shangoedi and her mob. The self-reliant characters in the book are nearly all men, the self-surrendering women. A rather trying obsessive fear of what Blake called female domination runs in fact through all Cary's work. It is most obvious in the relations of Gulley and Sara in *The Horse's Mouth*, where Cary makes thematic use of Blake's poem, 'The Mental Traveller'. It is perhaps worth noting that when that dominating female Sara first appears by name in Cary's writing, she is African – the central figure in an extraordinary fantasy which Cary must have written as early as his first tour in Nigeria and which is practically the only piece of writing of that period in his life that he thought worth keeping. It was while he was in Nigeria that he asserted, in a letter to his wife, that women were more cruel than men, and fonder of destruction; and *Aissa Saved* was begun at the time news of the Nigerian women's riots of 1929 was reaching the English newspapers. Viewed in this wide perspective, Carr's seeming 'conversion' at the beginning of *Aissa Saved* is a tragic abrogation of responsibility and ranks him with the characters of whom Cary writes in a manuscript note on the novel: 'Idea is that by this debauch they dodge responsibility, they throw it upon God and escape the burden of responsibility.' Carr's surrender to Mrs Carr is the exact counterpart to Ojo's connivance at the sacrifice of Aissa's child at the end of the book; Carr has in fact already failed in responsibility and sacrificed his own child by not sending the pregnant Mrs Carr to England. Ojo is first introduced to us as someone who might be either self-reliant or self-abandoning. We hear him conducting choir practice partly in the brisk and business-like tones of Carr doing a job of work ('No, no, dat's no good. *Can't* you listen?') and partly, when he repeats the words of the hymn, in the tone of 'a Mrs Carr rather drunk and hysterical, if that were possible' (p. 15). But the book's penultimate scene is a surrender, and Ojo bows down before Vala, the goddess Mystery. When Aissa prepares to sacrifice Abba, he at first thrusts himself among the frenzied worshippers, crying out that this is murder, just as Carr had tried to turn back the expedition to Kalu; but the sight of Aissa singing

> All de tings I lak de mos
> I sacrifice dem to his blood

overcomes the last vestige of his training:

Her joyful voice, her look of exaltation, the disfigurement of her face pierced Ojo to the soul. In that moment he perceived that she and Makoto were right and he was wrong. He had called them pagans because of their pagan rites – but their hearts were more Christian than his. He was fighting against the very spirit of love and sacrifice, against the wisdom of Jesus and the power of the Holy Ghost.

He fell on his knees before the woman and kissed her wounds.

(p. 208)

4

Aissa Saved, then, is a partisan, even a polemical book; its seeming objectivity reveals itself over the course of the novel as a grave, Swiftian irony at the expense of those who try to cast their burdens on the Lord. Cary's bias is confirmed by a drafted letter to his publisher, Ernest Benn, in which he says of the novel:

> It is not an attack on religion but an exposition of the effects of several kinds of education, ethical in Bradgate and Ali, materialist in Jacob, Christian in the Carrs and Aissa, pagan in others, Mohamedan in the Emir. It is however in one sense an attack on one kind of sacrifice. It seeks to show that the idea of sacrifice when removed from that of utility, of service, i.e. pleasing God, pleasing Oke, becomes pure juju and also self-indulgence. Thus Carr's conversion in the second chapter and Ojo's and Aissa's discovery in the last that to be happy it is only necessary to abandon personal responsibility and give up all to Christ, are critical points. These are in fact surrenders – escapes of human nature over-powered by the responsibility of judgement, of choosing, into the bosom of a nurse. (MS.)

'Attack' is a strong word, which exposes the book's doctrinaire intention. At times, it reads as if it had been written by Kipling's McAndrew. The imaginative impoverishment which results from this may be illustrated by the way Cary fails to sustain our interest in Ali or to make us believe in his martyrdom. He described Ali to his publisher as 'a Mohamedan in name, in ethics a public schoolboy'. Cary was never sympathetic to Islam, and one or two quotations from his letters which I have already given hint at his hostility to the

Moslem co-rulers of the North. For this reason Ali, in *Aissa Saved*, is deliberately, and rather unconvincingly, separated from his Moslem environment. The reader who protests that Ali's integrity might owe more to the Koran than the cricket field may seem as naïve as the woman who amused Cary by telling him, apropos of a later heroine, 'You do not understand Nina.' But we frequently do have such a feeling about a character in a novel; and it occurs whenever the vitality of the fable – the book's characters in action – has been circumscribed by the novelist's wish to expound a thesis.

Cary himself, in the preface to the Carfax edition, admitted that he had been too doctrinaire in *Aissa Saved*:

> Like anyone who has broken, with difficulty out of a confused foggy disintegrated state of feeling and thought into moderately clear going, I wanted to tell everyone how to find the road. I did not realise that everyone has his own fog, and therefore needs a special map; that most of those who wanted a way out had found it for themselves, and that the rest would rather stay where they were; that is, different people needed different kinds of faith; 'true' for them.   (p. 10)

Fortunately, the discovery was made before the book had reached its final form; and *Aissa Saved* escapes being a headmasterly discourse on the virtue of taking responsibility, thanks to Cary's imaginative and undoctrinaire portrayal of three of its characters.

Since there is a good deal of Cary himself in Bradgate, it is natural that the District Officer should be one of these characters whose presentation does not wholly conform to the novel's dichotomy between the sound and responsible on the one hand, and the unsound and irresponsible on the other. In his dealings with the Carrs, Bradgate's amiable ethic appears as nothing more than what Gerald Gould, in the only early review to grasp the book's clash of fundamental values, called 'sacred obtuseness'. Many of the book's disasters might have been averted if Bradgate had mentally crossed some of his bridges before he built them. His passion for the practical is several times presented as a way of evading fundamental issues. When after the first Kolu riot he writes Carr a 'good' letter of veiled reproaches accompanied by a gift of potatoes, and gets in return a rather more honest 'good' letter sent with some coals-of-fire tomatoes, Carr's shots go home

> because Bradgate suspected that he could not answer the question off hand, What are you really doing in Yanrin? What are you driving at? That the religious questions might after all be of some importance, that they might have some connexion with education, for instance, which he knew to be important. He suspected but he did not know because he did not want to know. He had no time to bother about such matters just now.
>
> (p. 113)

When Mrs Carr thinks of Bradgate as 'scuttling about like a rat in the dark', the image reflects on her own spiritual arrogance; but it is also a fair comment on Bradgate's myopic industry:

> Bradgate was of course a loyal son of the Church, for which he had filial love and respect, but he had not been to a service for thirty years, and he had even a vague notion that this abstinence was meritorious, that on the whole he showed himself a man of religious probity in not going, because he had another vague notion that the creed, if he ever had time to examine it and find out its real meaning, would not represent his own belief, whatever it was, when he had time to look into it.
>
> (p. 109)

Nor is this the only place in the book where doubt is cast on the thesis that the self-reliant are saved and the self-sacrificing are lost. Hilda Carr is a more interesting and complex character than Bradgate because, whereas Cary consciously modifies his presentation of the District Officer, Hilda Carr seems to escape her author's intentions entirely. 'Sacrifice', Cary wrote in another draft of his letter to Ernest Benn, 'is a fundamental doctrine of the Church and nearly all Churches, and where it is performed for a purpose . . . it is justified in its own frame of reference, Christian, pagan and so on. But where it is performed as a surrender of the will, as an escape, a suicide, a piece of self-indulgence it must be called wrong because it is a surrender of the personal responsibility which is the right and glory of mankind.' There are plenty of indications that Cary meant Hilda Carr's self-sacrifice to be what Blake termed 'the self-enjoyings of self-denial'. Carr, thinking of his wife among others, ponders the way that 'greed, lust and selfishness . . . could change their very being and appear as industry, love, chastity, and thoughtfulness' (p. 26). When Aissa vanishes into the throng at the pagan festival, Mrs Carr refuses to leave without her and is ready to be martyred on the spot, we are told, 'in revenge'.

But Cary's worst indictment of Hilda Carr is that, like Ishe and Aissa, she sacrifices her child. He was shocked on his arrival in Nigeria to find that the wives of missionaries remained in the country for their confinements at a time when malaria rendered a white child's chance of survival very small indeed. To Cary this represented an abandonment of a woman's chief responsibility, and he made it the theme of one of his best short stories, 'Government Baby'. Hilda Carr does not let go of life like Martha Smith; the novel rather implies that she sacrifices the one responsibility to another, her husband's work. But even here she is made to exemplify the selfishness of the extremely unselfish: 'he was certainly far from well, whatever he might say, and it was thoughtless of him to be worrying her to go home when he knew that he needed her. No doubt he would begin at breakfast when he found that she had been up these two hours. But if he did she would simply not answer. He was too stupid. Could he not see she was anxious about him?' (p. 150).

Yet for all Cary's exposure of Hilda Carr's petty unselfishnesses, he describes her moment of glory, which occurs just before the passage I have quoted, apparently without any of the irony that marks the description of her husband's ecstatic surrender to the irrational. Hilda's is a moment of victory, not surrender: 'She stood resting against the wall, and as she struggled for breath the crowing cocks in the boys' compound were like trumpets blowing for the triumph of her spirit.' There is no direct irony here. The question is whether or not there is oblique irony. Is Hilda the victim of illusion in thinking that she has saved Aissa?

Cary chose the titles of his novels with great care. They were, he once told his American publisher, essential parts of his books: 'I don't forget for a moment that they appear at the top of each page' (17 December 1947). *Aissa Saved*, as a title, is to a large degree ironic.

Aissa is not saved, in the crude sense that she is captured and killed when all her companions escape; and she is not saved in the subtler sense that the certainty of salvation she experiences in sacrificing Abba represents a loss of the real Aissa, the gay and sensual young woman who fights with every ruse in her power against the spirit which is prompting her to sacrifice her child. Cary's manuscript notes on the book suggest, however, that the title is by no means wholly ironic. 'Aissa herself not so plainly escapes', he writes; and, in another place: 'The end is the crux. Essentials of end Aissa moved by love of Jesus demanding all gives all, i.e. she gives up herself. Ojo gives up somebody else.' And the novel's close shows that Aissa loses her life to save it; in her agony she is again the anxious mother of Abba, whom she believes to be in Heaven and actually sees being given a ride on the Holy Goat. The book finally becomes much more than a satire on religious escapism, because both Hilda Carr and Aissa escape from Cary's directive irony.

The reason this came about is in part the fact that Cary took three years to write this short book – years, as the Carfax preface tells us, of continual self-exploration. During this time his interest shifted from ethics and Ali to enthusiasm and Aissa. That is to say, he came increasingly to feel that life demanded a faith and not a code, the spirit rather than the letter. In consequence, the doubts he cast on Bradgate's view of things are self-doubts; a schoolboy code of conduct seems inadequate to explain Ali; and Hilda and Aissa between them pull the whole argument about self-reliance and self-surrender completely out of shape. Another, and perhaps more influential reason why Cary's first novel escapes being a *roman à thèse* is that his choice of an African setting threw him back to a period in his life when his personal philosophy had not been as well-defined as it became in his forties. In Borgu, he had been the sole representative of one set of values among many social groups, each with values of its own. In such a situation the sensitive observer – missionary, administrator, or anthropologist – acquires a response to personality as such, independent of codes of behaviour. This response created the character of Aissa.

A novelist's imagination needs to be larger than his philosophy. Because of his determination not to publish before he had clarified his own beliefs, Cary was in real danger of producing a mummified image of life. It augured well for his future as a novelist that he was able to recall from earlier days the sensation of life recognizing itself, and use it to vitalize his first published story almost, it seems, in defiance of his own judgement.

A Pagan Man

I

Joyce Cary's method of composing 'over the whole surface at once like a picture' makes it impossible for anyone to sort out the manuscripts of his books into their successive versions. For each of his novels there has survived a confused pile of manuscript in which the rejected material is far bulkier than the final typescript. According to the severer school of critics, this rejected material should stay where it is, in the discard. The argument seems to be that if a sculptor mishews his stone we can't mend matters by gathering up the chippings. But while a scrutiny of manuscript material can never alter our evaluation of a novel, it can throw welcome light on the writer's development; and this is especially true of Cary's second novel, *An American Visitor*, which was published in 1933.

The surplus manuscript portions of *An American Visitor* are of three kinds. Some of them were left out because they were irrelevant to the book's theme. Except so far as this kind of material explains (without justifying) the presence of a number of ghost characters in the book, it can be left out of our considerations also. Other portions were rejected for the opposite reason that they were over-relevant. Because he was afraid of making the theme of a book too explicit, Cary was ruthless in his excision of such passages. But taken together with the third kind of material – Cary's self-directions and overt statements of the book's theme – they are of great value to us in showing what were his intentions in this novel.

The jottings which define the book's theme include a synopsis which Cary perhaps intended for his publisher:

In this story of a modern American girl with the political and religious prejudices of her time and country, we see a passionate love affair and a religious creed growing on the same root as a political idea; each the necessary and complementary expression of the same personality, which is itself characteristic of a national atmosphere. The story of Maria Hasluck is therefore a commentary and sidelight upon American civilization and its preoccupations; but as she moves in a British dependency, falls in love with a British official and is involved therefore in local politics, the action raises also urgent and important questions of imperial policy and development.

(MS.)

If we leave aside for the present the question of whether or not it is the novelist's business to raise questions of imperial policy, we see that Cary intended Marie Hasluck to be, as the title of the book implies, his first concern. *An American Visitor* begins and ends with Marie. It starts with people asking what she is doing and what does she want. It ends with her kneeling at Bewsher's grave, an action that symbolizes the way she has both found and lost what she really wants: 'I'm not praying, but where Monkey is, the ground feels kind of different.'

What Marie wants is security: the kind of security a child feels in his own world of love. In the corrupt adult world Marie thinks such security exists among the Birris of Nigeria, whom she idealizes into perfect children of nature:

> Marie wants love to rule the world. She wants a world without grief and sorrow, ruin, injustice and despair, and she knows she can't have it, at first. She wants happiness for herself and everyone else.
>
> (MS.)
>
> The story is about 1. Mahrie's desire that Gawd shld rule – and her conversion to that belief under pressure of her love for Monkey and the Birri. It shews that she wants God to rule and therefore the pressure and the sources of the desire that God should rule – and that his rule should be one of love – it is the refuge of all those terrified by the wickedness and cruelty of the world ... (the palm without the dust).
>
> (MS.)

It is Marie's love of goodness, beauty and truth which makes her desire the golden, the escape – she doesn't admit that they are flowers of battle. ... For love, she has the golden age idea – she can't bear to think of the

Birri vulgarized and beneath that, of the world in danger – no peace anywhere – this is at Nok.

(MS.)

A phrase which occurs several times in the manuscript, always in association with Marie, is 'the everlasting arms'. When, at the beginning of the book, the A.D.O., Gore, comes to her help in getting on to the steamer and so down the river to Nok, she exclaims, 'Aren't you just the everlasting arms?' This encounter was too good to jettison, because it establishes the poles on which the whole tale moves: the readiness of people like Marie to cast all their burdens on the Lord and the refusal of people like Gore, who find life a long and weary battle, to trust anything to luck or to Providence.

It is true that in the first part of the story Marie is enough of a rationalist to protest to Gore about the quietism of those who, like the missionary, Dobson, leave everything to the Almighty: 'But you're not really Church any more than Monkey. You would be ashamed to ask anyone else to do your job for you' (MS. Cf. pp. 129-30). But such an attitude barely conceals Marie's underlying need for stability and certainty, her distress that there is 'nothing secure, nothing fixed, permanent and trustworthy in the whole world'. Her cynicism is a surface ripple which betrays this undertow: 'Even her cynicism, which abused the world for not being governed by the finer feelings was sentimental' (MS.).

In the ninth chapter of *An American Visitor*, this strong current of Marie's nature takes a new direction. In spite of the efforts made by the District Officer, Bewsher, to keep them out, the anthropologist, Marie, and the tin-prospector, Cottee, have found their way several-ly into the Birri reserve, and already the tribe is disturbed. The four chief characters, Bewsher, Cottee, Marie and Gore, are brought together in the Nok resthouse. Marie rapidly falls in love with Bewsher. In this, as in all her other enthusiasms, the driving force is her craving for security. Her trust in the Birri as children of nature has been shaken by the events of the preceding afternoon, during which Bewsher has narrowly escaped being eviscerated by one of the more uninhibited members of the tribe. Bewsher's affection for the Birri and his determination to protect them from the ills of civilization reassure Marie and help her to suppress her own misgivings. She does not see that Bewsher's protectiveness has rather different motives from her own. Meanwhile, Cottee's irritation at not being allowed to prospect inside the Nok reserve is being exacerbated by his jealousy of Bewsher's success with Marie. Gore tries as usual to keep the peace and effect a compromise between the parties, as a good working political officer should; but, with a sudden characteristic swing from indolence to decisive action, Bewsher expels the prospectors from the division, and escapes from the wrath of his Resident by disappearing with Marie into the remotest parts of the reserve.

The next time Marie appears in the story, Bewsher is her lover and she is luxuriating in her new security:

> This happiness which seemed so extraordinary to her; this new kind of experience in which she moved awkwardly and doubtfully like a child at her first party was not a holiday, an escape from daily endurances, but life itself. It could not come to an end because it was natural and real, the right kind of living. To love and be loved. . . .
>
> She gave herself up to confidence, to security, to delight with the same feeling of luxury with which she indulged her passion for the man.

(pp. 115–16)

This confidence has a surprising setting. Marie is patrolling the outskirts of the Dobsons' mission compound which is actually surrounded, as she has already half sensed, by hundreds of Birri resolved on killing Bewsher. Thanks more to Bewsher himself than to the troops Marie has summoned from the divisional headquarters, the attack is repulsed. A few months later, Marie marries Bewsher, and her security would appear to be complete. But in fact her fundamental misgivings, strengthened by the Birris' treachery, grow worse. Her plan to persuade Monkey to retire fails, and within a few days of the wedding he is back in the reserve, allegedly surrounded by tribesmen and the subject of much debate at Alo on whether or not a rescue party should be sent in. For Marie waiting at Alo there are, as one draft puts it, 'no everlasting arms underneath her only a damned old crooked universe':

Marie is all the time aware of impermanence – what's the good of anything – one damn thing after another – and this is what makes her sad –
even after Monkey shows her how to live . . . At last her sense of insecurity
is too much for her – and she's converted.

As in *Aissa Saved*, this religious conversion is the reaction from a
hysterically violent outburst against the injustice which makes life
insecure. Women like Marie, Cottee remarks in one draft version,
'pass so quickly from the joyful contemplation of goodness in
things to believing that goodness exists independently of things –
that they don't know the difference'. So Marie moves from the
knowledge that love can cast out fear, as it did in the first attack on
the mission, to the illusion that love can dispel the source of fear.
She casts her last and greatest care – for Monkey's safety – on the
Lord, and hides Monkey's gun at the moment he realizes he must
shoot. In this, as she admits afterwards, she is relying only on 'the
oldest kind of juju'. Her name is deliberately chosen by Cary: Marie
trusts to luck, stakes all on a sustaining goodness which is not really
there.

2

Joyce Cary's intentions in his portrayal of Marie Hasluck are
clear in the book and emphatic in the manuscript. Yet he did not
manage to bring her to life. Whereas even such minor English
characters of *An American Visitor* as the youthful war veteran,
Stoker, have a historical solidity about them, it is hard to conceive
of any American anthropologist who, in 1923 (roughly the year of
the book's events), could be as naïve as Marie about the joys of
primitive life. Certainly no one who spoke the Birris' language as
well as Marie is supposed to do could entertain such illusions about
them. It is true that Cary intended Marie to have a kind of insub-
stantiality; in comparison with the other European characters
(excepting Cottee), she was to appear detribalized. But since most
New Englanders have very strong tribal sanctions, this was a fault of
observation. Moreover, in so far as Marie has any substance as a

character, it is undermined by the novelist's resentment (for it amounts to that) of her influence over Bewsher. The Blakean theme of female domination, already rampant in *Aissa Saved*, persists in *An American Visitor*. Marie begins to destroy Bewsher when she tries to make him retire from Africa; the Birris are his life.

An American Visitor is in fact Bewsher's book. Its eponymous heroine is less sympathetic and interesting than Cary meant her to be, because Bewsher steals the show. Marie is put together from theories, some of them of recent formation, about national character and the natures of women. But Bewsher had been alive for thirty years in Cary's imagination. The statement that he has been in the country for fifteen years at the time of the book's events makes him one of Lugard's original Northern Residents – 'the old gang who had ruled Nigeria like independent despots', as they appeared to the next generation of administrators, typified by Gore (p. 41). We have already seen the profound impression these pioneers made on Joyce Cary when he first went to Nigeria. Although he assured his publisher that he was careful to avoid any possible identification of his characters with the men he had known in Nigeria, he puts a good deal of his admiration for T. F. Carlyle into his portrait of Bewsher. One of Cary's contemporaries in the Political Service spotted the likeness immediately: 'I wondered whether some at least of the exploits of the District Officer – e.g. his sudden unaccompanied visits to trouble spots – might not be based on Carlyle's unexpected appearances, days ahead of his carriers and escort, in the then unsettled pagan area of Tangale-Waja in the south of Gombe Division.'[1] In early portions of the manuscript the name of the pagan tribe, whom Cary eventually called the Birri, is the Tall, after the name of the district inhabited by Carlyle's Tangale; and in other rejected portions, Bewsher repeatedly cites Carlyle's dealings with the Tangale as his guide in ruling the Birri. The association is also made in a manuscript passage of *The African Witch*, which states that 'Sangster was a

---

[1] E. S. Pembleton. The setting of the novel is not, however, Gombe, but the right bank of the Niger south of Lokoja. It is roughly localized by Cary in a sketch map in the manuscript.

good pagan man, but unlike Bewsher of —— or Carlyle of Tangale he had never done anything to make them richer or to develop their government.'

There were in fact many kinds of pagan men; but they all had in common the determination to preserve their own tribe from the encroachments of more 'advanced' peoples. The type was familiar enough once upon a time to give rise to the joke among educated Nigerians that if ever they went away, tribal warfare would break out among the British. All pagan men fascinated Cary. Cock Jarvis, who was in many ways the prototype of Bewsher – like Bewsher, he is entirely absorbed and happy in his work and quite unaware that he is an object of pity to the rest of the world – had been the administrator of an Emirate, not a pagan division; but when Cary expanded his career for the unpublished sequels to *Castle Corner*, he turned him into a pagan man, and in so doing tried to explain the appeal the pagans had for English administrators:

> At that time, nobody took much interest in the pagans; or their jujus. Officials, even junior officials, or missionaries, destroyed them every day. The only difference was that the missionaries did so on religious grounds and officials on political grounds. It was understood that the Emirs had a right to be Mohamedans; and to build mosques; but the pagans must not be pagans. However, most of the men who heard Jarvis at once began to sympathize with him. It was as though something in them had been waiting for this moment to come out on the pagan side. In fact, most of the officials had no religious policy; and their own religion was instinctive or purely ethical. This is why their sympathies, the natural sympathies of the Englishman for all that is old and therefore full of associations, having first been engaged for the Emirates, now rose to support the pagans; and even the juju places.
>
> ... Laka was wife and children to him; home and religion. His imagination caught hold of this matter, so congenial to its desires, and created of it something so grand and imposing that the dullest people, hearing the description of Laka and its ancient religion, its wise customs, its noble people, were affected; and carried about Nigeria the notion that somewhere down the Niger there was a tribe of unusual quality; altogether a good lot of chaps.

This passion for the unspoilt pagan was nearly always accompanied

by a contempt for the Westernized African. Cary was well aware
of the unfairness of this partisanship, which he had himself shared
for a time, and he satirized it in an entertaining sketch called 'A
Pagan Man'. This story, which is unpublished, has for subject a
District Officer who jealously guards his tribe from such corrupting
influences as education and Christianity. When he falls ill amongst
them, they display little interest in the matter, and he would be left
to die were it not for the skill and courage of his Yoruba clerk, who
tends him and succeeds in getting him to hospital; but at the end of
the story the pagan man is still abusing the upstart Southerners and
praising the fine fellows of his special tribe. Some of this satirical
attitude shows itself in the manuscript's earliest presentation of
Bewsher's character:

> And now they were going to be turned into a lot of damned coast apes,
> money-grabbers whose highest distinction was to have cash in the bank,
> whose glory was to do other fellows in a deal and who considered
> politeness among themselves or consideration for others not only a waste
> of time but actually despicable, a confession of inferiority. . . . It was true
> that pagan men generally, as they were called, nearly always took this
> attitude, strongly pro-pagan and anti-coast. But none of them was as
> violent as Bewsher.

In fact, Bewsher is in every way a more violent character in the
early stages of the novel, more conspicuous in his drinking and
swearing, and given to rather Edwardian jokes; a period piece, as
Cottee still calls him in the finished book. Cary seems to have felt
some such view of his pagan man was a necessary brake on an
enthusiasm which threatened, in the book's early stages, to run
away with him altogether in such passages as the following:

> Bewsher had called him a pagan man and by that he had meant not a
> trickster who won cheap glory by risking his life to no advantage, but one
> who put first his duty to the people in his charge, and would throw away
> for them not just his life which cost him nothing to lose, but his friends
> and his health which would cost a great deal, even his career. Grayson
> knew that Bewsher had sacrificed his own career to the Birri.

The Grayson of this passage, ultimately to be replaced in the book by
Gore, was an eager, anxious, monocled young man indistinguish-

able from the Evelyn Corner of Cary's soldiering sketches: in fact, Cary himself. And Bewsher as Cary first depicted him was one of the 'old gang' as they appeared to Cary's generation, eccentric yet magnificent. The same attitude of hero-worship tempered with a self-defensive mockery underlies the saying current at the time Cary went to Nigeria, that Lugard had recruited his Residents from the Twelve Apostles and the Forty Thieves. Accordingly, Bewsher in the published book is often presented to us as a saint with a strong dash of the brigand. Yet while Cary, in 1932, could recapture the admiration he had once felt for Carlyle and other pagan men as people, he could no longer share their ideals as administrators. Consequently, a good deal of the book is taken up with oblique criticisms of Bewsher's aims.

3

Bewsher's chief aim as an administrator is 'to preserve and develop the rich kind of local life which is the essence and the only justification of nationalism' (p. 133). He knows just what he has to do. First the tribes must be unified into the All-Birri and given a code of laws based on their own principles of justice. Then the traders may come in; but not the missions – 'that would be putting the pike in the pond' – because they would undermine the tribes' own religion, which should be preserved and purified:

> When Bewsher was in high spirits about his work and especially the future prospects of his work he had a trick of cocking his head to one side and contemplating the air with a victorious grin, as if he could see there already complete the magnificent vision of a Birri civilization, self-conscious and proud, enjoying all modern hygienic advantages without modern self-indulgence, sportsmen still but also peaceful, rid of foolish and cruel superstition but not irreligious or materialistic, keeping their nakedness but not their poverty, their independence but not the cruel egotism and selfishness of European nationalism.
>
> (MS.)

When Cary described *An American Visitor* to his former senior officer in Bauchi, H. S. W. Edwardes, he instinctively stated its theme from Bewsher's point of view: 'a pagan tribe attacked by civilization in its two most insidious forms; social and religious' (2 January 1934). For Bewsher's vision of the All-Birri was the kind of ideal held by many of the pioneer administrators of Nigeria. The most influential and eloquent of them all, at the time Cary went to Africa, was the then Lieutenant-Governor of the North, Charles Temple. Cary was enthusiastic about Temple's *Native Races and their Rulers*, published in 1918, and wrote home to ask his wife to buy a copy. It is still an absorbingly lively and interesting book. But the mid-century reader finds himself marvelling at the double-think of its contents as well as of its title. The astonishing thing is that anyone with Temple's admiration for the shrewdness and enterprise of individual Africans could have believed that Western civilization could be measured out to the continent by the spoonful; that people would remain in docile subjection to the Imperial power while at the same time developing their own institutions to the point at which a token independence might be granted by the former conqueror.

In saying this we are, of course, being wise after the event. Cary had the insight to be wise before it. *An American Visitor* was written at the time when he first became critical of the old protective colonial policy of ensuring that people continued to live as they had always lived, though within the bounds of law and order. Although *Aissa Saved* got in a few digs at the way this policy was administered, it did not criticize the policy as such; indeed, the earlier book might be said to have stemmed from the protective jealousy aroused in Cary in 1919 when he heard that a missionary had entered his division. But *Aissa Saved* was begun before the Labour Government of 1929 to 1931 introduced new aims in colonial administration. By 1932, when he wrote *An American Visitor*, Cary was clear in his own mind about the need for a new approach in place of the old *laisser faire* attitude, and he had the confidence of knowing that there were many who shared his views. This meant that in his presentation of the old-style administrator, Bewsher, his heart was at variance with his head. His real problem in the book was to find ways of 'placing' Bewsher critically, from a political point of view, without sacrificing any of the enthusiasm for Carlyle and other pagan men which had been the book's original driving force.

One device Cary adopts for making us view Bewsher critically is the use he makes of the pagans themselves, the Birri. Unlike the Africans of *Aissa Saved*, the Birri of *An American Visitor* are kept in the middle distance. We may at first be deceived into thinking their role is a passive one, to illustrate the varying attitudes towards them of the Europeans in the novel: that they are there to be idealized by Marie, served by Gore, converted by Dobson, exploited by Cottee, occasionally shot by Stoker and intermittently governed by Bewsher. But a jotting among the drafts shows that Cary intended them to have an important part in the story: 'Main story must be whole question of Europeanizing – segregating, encouraging national spirit (which Monkey is doing and which kills him).' As in Cary's first novel, there are many parallels between the African and the European parts of the book.

The strongest of all these parallels is that drawn between Bewsher and the tribe he serves. This is made very clear in one of the superfluous portions of the manuscript, when Marie tells Bewsher that the reason he is so fond of the Birris is that he is so like them:

> Bewsher gave the point a moment's consideration. But it was too fantastic to confuse a naked Birri with the melancholy, sophisticated Gore or even with himself. Besides, he knew why he liked the Birri. They were a people whose values were sound. They admired good things like courage, generosity, forebearance, fine manners, and they detested bad things like boasting, ostentation, rudeness, disrespect for age and authority.

Bewsher, that is, makes the fatal mistake of judging the whole tribe by himself; and his idealised picture of the Birri contrasts sharply with their collective and individual behaviour as it is presented to us in the course of the book. A passage in one of Cary's notebooks, though written at a later date, suggests what he was attempting in these scenes:

The romantic notion of a tribe as a place of brotherly love is nonsense. Africans are very affectionate people. In Nigeria I used to see my sergeants walking about hand in hand, tough old veterans who had fought with Lord Kitchener at Ondurman – on the other side. But that good nature and affectionate feeling is racial and not tribal. People write of the tribal dances, and hunts, as signs of fraternity. More rows and fights and murders come from the dances and hunts than anything else. I don't mean that the dances are bad, only that they are not scenes of fraternal community, but of mass excitement which is quite a different thing.

(N85)

In the reserve, this mass excitement which powers the first attack upon Bewsher is opposed by the responsible Obai, who is abused on all sides for his lack of community spirit. Here the parallel between the black and white communities is very marked. The Birri when they relax and enjoy a sense of tribal solidarity before the fight are exactly in the mood of the small group of English officers when they wait at Alo for the order to march to Bewsher's rescue. Obai's counterpart at Alo is Gore, whose lonely sense of responsibility has already been contrasted with the abandon of the tribal beer-feast (p. 84). It is ironical that when Obai first comes to Bewsher's help on his own initiative he should be looked at askance by Gore as well as Stoker because of his failure to back up his own side.

Bewsher's first mistake is to think the Birri tribe will ever consist of people like Obai, that is, people like himself. His second error is to overlook the disruption which the modern world has already brought into the Nok reserve. As so often happens, the story shows what the rejected parts of the manuscript baldly state. We are told in the drafts that 'Bewsher had broken [the authority of the chiefs] when he would not allow the old punishments for witchcraft and adultery; when he picked out young chiefs from their age class for special education and promotion; when he dug latrines and brought in new kinds of farming, new crops, irrigation, new medicines for fever and smallpox'. In the published novel this point is made when Uli, sent to Berua by Bewsher, returns with a knowledge not only of irrigation, but of Hausa sexual customs, which are outlandish to the pagans; and so becomes infected with a sense of guilt which turns him into a trouble-maker.

Once again the point is driven home by the way Cary makes a parallel use of the English and African parts of the story. Uli's frantic bewilderment after he has broken the taboos of the tribe is similar to Marie's moments of despair; and like her he seeks escape in a conversion which is really a flight from responsibility – in his case, into the exhilarating license of the mission compound. But like another misfit, Cottee, Uli finds that this uncharted freedom tires, and both men welcome the war for the chance it gives each of them to slip back into the tribe. A similarity between Cottee and Uli is in fact established quite early in the book, when Cottee's brief spying on Bewsher and Marie – the perpetual outsider's envious glimpse of the committed – is repeated in Uli's watch on them at the mission. The thought at the back of Uli's mind then – 'I've got to look out for myself for no one else will' – is always in Cottee's. Both Cottee and Uli do well out of the war, as does another detribalized Birri character, Marie's servant, Henry. An early draft established the resemblance between Cottee and Henry by making Marie tell Cottee that, like Henry, he was an adept at 'getting away with things'. Both compensate for their alienation from the tribe by adopting the pose of the mellow and detached philosopher. Both end up exploiting the Birri by giving them what they consider they ought to want: illicit gin and abortions in Henry's store or employment in Cottee's mine.

Cottee, like the Birri, is a device for getting Bewsher into political perspective. His criticisms of colonial paternalism are often Cary's own: 'It does seem rather strange that we won't let these poor devils have any of the comforts and conveniences that we couldn't do without ourselves. . . . Why, we don't even teach them English. We behave exactly as if English books and English ideas would poison them' (p. 97). Through Cottee's eyes we see that Bewsher's death saves him from witnessing the inevitable destruction of the Birri tribe, and of many other tribes, that had to precede the construction of larger and (to Bewsher's class and generation) less admirable loyalties. Cary uses Cottee as his mouthpiece in criticizing the old colonialism, but he safeguards our affection for Bewsher by making Cottee as unpleasant as possible. As Marie says, whether Cottee is right or wrong about the Birri, he is wrong in himself. Bewsher does the historically doomed thing from the best motives; Cottee, an intellectual of long views, collaborates with the forces of history for the worst of reasons.

Because he is a device rather than a person, Cottee fails to carry conviction as a character. His reflections grow wearisome, and threaten to turn the book into a study of colonialism rather than a novel. This is to say, the struggle to get his colonial pioneer into focus, which had already resulted in Cary abandoning *Cock Jarvis*, nearly wrecked his second novel. Fortunately, he realized in the course of writing *An American Visitor* that Bewsher's quality had to consist in something other than his policy for the Birri, which was outdated; even something other than the class and tradition to which he belonged, for they too might be held to have had their day. Whether Bewsher was right or wrong about the Birri, he had to be right in himself. He needed to be made the expression of an attitude to life which Cary was coming to feel had inherent value, quite apart from the historically conditioned actions to which it might give rise. In exploring this profounder and more personal quality of the typical pagan man, Cary grasped a clue which he was to follow in subsequent and perhaps better novels.

4

Just as Cottee and the Birri are used to place Bewsher in his political aspect, so Gore and Marie serve as foils for the portrayal of Bewsher's personal faith. At first the contrast between Bewsher and Gore may appear to be part of the book's political theme: a contrast between two notions of indirect rule which were particularly sharp when Cary went to Nigeria in 1914. The conflict was over the individual officer's responsibility. Temple thought the man in

the bush should be given an entirely free hand; Lugard, alarmed
after some years' absence to find how the independent powers of
the District Officers had increased, wanted more control to be
exercised by the central Secretariat. In the novel, Gore, with his
strong respect for Service orders and his sense of the chain of responsibility running from Whitehall to the bush, is Lugard's ideal
political officer; the portrait of Bewsher, on the other hand, owes
much to the lively pochade of a pioneer administrator in Temple's
book about indirect rule. Gore's unhappy task is to conciliate the
tin-licensing authorities at the capital whenever the actions of
Bewsher, who regards Nok and the Birri as entirely his personal
and private concern, become particularly high-handed, But the
difference between the two men is much more than a contrast of
administrative theory. It is a contrast in attitudes to life.

Cary's manuscripts show that it took him some time to evolve an
A.D.O. who really could assist in the realization of Bewsher as a
character. We have seen that in the earliest drafts Gore was Joyce
Cary in 1914, anxious to prove himself worthy of the magnificent
chief to whom he had been assigned. When the decision had to be
taken whether or not to send troops to rescue Bewsher, Gore
discovered 'for the first time the loneliness of the man in authority',
especially in 'real circumstances complicated and ambiguous as only
reality can be'. In desperation, he hit on the plan of going himself
single-handed to Bewsher's aid. The Resident objected. 'He therefore found himself unable to use this escape, the martyr's and the
mystic's escape, from the burden of solving the intractable kind of
problems of which life, from the ruler's point of view, seemed to
be composed.' This presentation of Gore served the purpose of
emphasizing one of the book's contrasts; between the mystic's
approach to problems (exemplified in the Dobsons) and the prag-
matist's, as represented by Bewsher. But Cary soon realized that
Gore ought to contrast with Bewsher and not be dependent upon
him. The next move was to make him older. In one version he is
exactly the age Cary himself would have been had he stayed in
Nigeria till 1923. This detached Gore from Bewsher, whom he no

longer worshipped as a hero, but not from his inventor. The detachment was complete only when Cary hit on the idea of making him a
young man disillusioned by the war, and so without any of
Bewsher's Edwardian buoyancy. This Gore of the final novel is,
like Bewsher, a man accustomed to responsibility, and the scenes at
Alo, where he appears to Cottee and Stoker a helpless bureaucrat,
unable to take decisive action, are sharply ironic: he is in fact the
only man who is behaving responsibly in the circumstances,
because he knows, as the others do not, what the administrative
consequences of violence are likely to be.

But while both Gore and Bewsher are eternally vigilant, Gore's
vigilance is that of a sentry and Bewsher's that of a relaxed animal
that can spring to activity at the first scent of danger. Gore is saddled
with responsibility; Bewsher rides it. Whereas the pagans have
their beer-feasts and Bewsher his Sunday feeling, Gore is tempera-
mentally unable to have a day off. When he goes on a quiet river
trip to escort a pagan deputation back to Nok, he finds himself
faced with the responsibility of preventing a riot which is unprevent-
able. He is no sooner aboard the *Black Swan* and relaxing in three
inches of muddy Niger than he is called upon by the prospectors to
solve their problems. Wherever there are people, Gore's nature and
training conspire to make him shoulder responsibility for them. He
can relax only in sleep, on leave in lonely hotels, and in a catastrophe;
such acts of God as hurricanes are the only events which make the
lugubrious Gore laugh, because they render his vigilance futile. He
is in short, a man who lives by rule, whereas Bewsher lives by faith.
Gore is an Anglo-Catholic; Bewsher, a born Protestant. What
gives the portrayal of Gore depth and dignity is his awareness of
inadequacy in his ordered life, an awareness that Cary was to
develop in the character of Wilcher in *To be a Pilgrim*. In his wistful
remark, 'My vicar at home tells me religion is rejoicing', there is a
regret for the unattainable which recurs in his dealings with Marie:
'She gave and then you wanted to give. You didn't give because
you hadn't the time and because she had a husband, but the desire
to give was itself a happiness so keen and unexpected that all at

once you found life extremely interesting and even admirable'
(p. 184).

But Bewsher gives all the time. Whereas Gore craves, but never
allows himself to get, freedom from responsibility, Bewsher feels
that responsibility is itself a freedom. Every event presents him
with a new set of circumstances which elicits a fresh response. He is
a pagan man not only because he responds to the Birris' love of
tradition, but because he shares their ability to live each moment
fully. Indeed, this freshness of response is the natural corollary of a
sense of tradition, because those who are most sure of their values
are most free to take decisions as the occasion arises. As one unused
passage put it:

> To Bewsher life was a kind of art in which each set of circumstances
> demanded the appropriate conduct, not the same conduct, but conduct
> fitting the moment, the situation and the people concerned. A great man
> was one whose actions had an exquisite kind of fitness and brilliance. A
> small man was one who originated nothing of his own but rolled along
> the bottom of circumstances like a pebble in a stream.

Bewsher's irruption into the story, leaping from a dugout on to the
lower deck of the *Black Swan*, has just this kind of *panache* about it,
and evokes from Marie the tribute due to a skilled performance:
'Wasn't that just beautiful?' (p. 38).

In the practice of this art of living, Bewsher's genius exists, like
Wordsworth's in his pagan days, 'by interchange of peace and
exaltation'. He is associated, at this first appearance on the river, with
the pagan boatman baling out his canoe with 'a gesture of joy and
mastery', and he shares also the pagans' capacity for complete
relaxation. The book's forward, linear movement is deliberately
made one of vigilance alternating with repose. The pattern established on the river-steamer – the long, tranquil day between the
violent excitement of embarking and disembarking – repeats itself
in the beer-feast between the first threat to Bewsher and the attack
on the Goshi mission, and again in the party at Alo between
Bewsher's escape from the massed tribesmen at Paré and the Birris'
last attack. Bewsher's enjoyment of the Alo party is as thorough as

the pagans' enjoyment of their beer-feast. It is the other Europeans who take thought for the morrow and despair. 'What pagans,' says the listening Moslem messenger when he is given a translation of 'Pack up your troubles'; and this pagan capacity Bewsher has for living in the moment is emphasized in one early version in which Uli runs away with his totem-mate Osana and (like Bewsher with Marie) takes refuge in the mission, where the lovers lie happily together, listening to the threatening drums of the outraged tribesmen.

The scenic settings of the book help this presentation of life as an alternation of periods of repose with periods of vigilance, each of which demands a new assessment and a new response. Joyce Cary is probably the least picturesque of all the English novelists who have written about the tropics. Yet the reader retains from *An American Visitor* a series of pictures in vivid chiaroscuro: the moonlight in the clearing of Nok village, when Uli and Obai return to it; the late afternoon sun on the river when the warriors are relaxing with their children before the renewed attack on Bewsher; the flares and camp-fires of the Alo mobilization; and, most vivid of all, the clearing round Goshi mission which stands exposed by moonlight to the attackers massed in the shadows of the wooded river valley. Cary's experience of bush fighting in 1915 gave special force to this symbolism of clearing and forest. So too did his lonely and often apprehensive days in Borgu, when the sudden sight of the Niger at its full width under an early morning sky would lift his heart with a memory of Lough Foyle shining in the tranquil Irish landscape. But Cary associated Ireland as well as Africa with latent treachery. The clearing, with its Beulah light, represents an interlude of peace in an endless war, made sweeter by the proximity of danger: 'It is fear that makes love, it is danger that makes joy' (MS.).

This is the kind of tranquillity that Marie enjoys with Bewsher at the mission before the pagans make their first attack on it. But when she and Monkey are again together at Goshi, after their marriage, the clearing with its vulnerable buildings becomes the symbol of a false security based on the illusion that evil does not exist

(Marie has been flirting with Christian Science) or that it is powerless against good, as she will believe after her sudden 'conversion' to the Dobsons' views. She likes to pretend the forest is not there:

> It was Marie's habit everywhere she went to take an early morning walk while Bewsher tackled his letters. Especially she looked forward to her walks in Goshi, which was the biggest clearing in the division. . . . Marie had learnt to hate the forest, not only because she saw in every mile of it an ambush waiting for Bewsher, but because its terrors made it impossible for her to be at peace within herself. When he was in the bush she was always preoccupied by mean fears of which she was ashamed.
>
> (pp. 210-11)

Marie is trying to secure Monkey's superannuation in order that the two of them, together with the child she is carrying, may always live in the clearing. But Monkey could not enjoy his 'Sunday feeling', with its recollections of his Devonshire home, if he was to be condemned to a life of Sundays in Devonshire. The passing watchman's humming of *'Ein feste burg ist unser Gott'* belongs to Sunday; Monkey is as unwilling to retreat permanently into that stronghold as he is to stay in Stoker's fort. Because of her inability to live, like Monkey, in the present, Marie takes refuge in the past as well as the future. Monkey has stopped a massacre single-handed and unarmed on the occasion of the first attack on the mission, so she trusts him to do it again. But the whole point of this seeming duplication is that life does not repeat itself. A situation in which Obai is Bewsher's opponent and not his ally calls for a quite different response; and, robbed of the means to the action that this new situation demands, Monkey is killed.

Bewsher in fact can only exist as an artist of action in a bad and unstable world; this is what Marie realizes too late:

> I just started right away trying to find a safe place for him even if I ruined his life and broke his heart. And when I couldn't get Monkey safe out of Birri I just had to have Birri safe for Monkey. But I didn't see that if Birri was safe, Monkey wouldn't be Monkey, and if the world was meant to be a safe place there wouldn't be any men like Monkey, and if no one was to die or suffer there wouldn't be any love, and if no one was to get killed there wouldn't be any life worth living.
>
> (p. 237)

This is much too explicit. In fact the weakness of the novel is that Cary, especially in the later chapters, goes on grinding his axe long after we have acknowledged its edge. The reason for this is that he realized that his admiration for Carlyle and others had given great weight to the politico-historical element in the book, and thence sought to redress the balance by overstating Bewsher's unique quality: his delight in responsibility not as a yoke but as the opportunity for creative living, for the mastery of each new situation. The novel in consequence becomes a demonstration; it lacks real conflict. Marie's flight from responsibility and Gore's servitude to it are not full counter-statements to Bewsher's way of life. The way the argument is weighted on Bewsher's side is seen when Marie finally decides not to give him his gun. She is not really leaving things to luck or Providence. Without wishing it, she is rising to the occasion in her own way, facing a situation that (to quote the Carfax preface) 'has to be dealt with imaginatively, by a creative effort of the mind'. Ironically, we are told: 'Marie accepted her responsibility' (p. 227).

At a later stage, Cary could have depicted Marie as fully and sympathetically as he depicted the nest-building Sara, and made Gore as complex and credible as Wilcher, without diverting sympathy from the pilgrim soul, the creator, Bewsher. But it is doubtful if he could have done this within the pages of a single book. Bewsher's supremacy weakens *An American Visitor* as a novel, but it gave Cary a double opportunity; to express his delight in the men of an earlier generation who had ruled a large territory with resourcefulness and finesse, and to exemplify in one of them the attitude to life which Cary himself had come to feel was the only sound response to its fundamental injustice.

A Jealous God

I

The usual disclaimer, 'Characters and scenes in this book are fictitious', was expanded in Joyce Cary's third novel, *The African Witch*, into an insistence that the women's war in the book should not be taken to refer in any way to the women's wars of the period in Southern Nigeria: 'The book has been written as a work of imagination, and not as a picture of contemporary conditions in West Africa.' Reviewers found this disingenuous. Certainly the presence among Joyce Cary's papers of a copy of the official enquiry into the Aba riots of 1929 suggests that there was a strong connexion between these incidents and the women's war in *The African Witch*. Like the witch, Elizabeth, the leaders of the Aba women used leaves carried from village to village for the purposes of their mobilization. The Aba women's declaration that 'the District Officer was born of a woman, and as they were women, they were going to see him', becomes the song of the women in the novel. And the official inquiry ended, as it does in the book, with censure of the unfortunate District Officer who felt compelled to fire into the crowd of frenzied women who 'believed themselves possessed of the spirit of womanhood and so inviolable'.[1]

The setting of *The African Witch* is not, however, Southern Nigeria, but a Northern Emirate. Although Cary claimed in a letter to his publisher that Rimi could not be identified with any one area in the North, his notes on the earlier stages of the novel show that at first he based Rimi town on Nafada 'with larger riverside population and pagan reserve' and later identified it with Lokoja. If Rimi town is Lokoja, Rimi kingdom approximates to that of the

[1] M. R. Perham: *Native Administration in Nigeria*, pp. 207, 209, 214.

Igbirra, whose traditional ruler was until very recently a pagan (like the Emir in the novel) and not, as is usual in Emirates, a Moslem. Scenically considered, Rimi is Lokoja; but its small European community owes much to Cary's memories of Nafada, and especially of the months he spent there as O.C. Troops in 1916 to 1917. The polo he organized at Nafada supplied Cary with the basis of a chapter in *The African Witch* which is modelled on the comic contests in Dickens and Surtees.

Cary has, however, a more ambitious model for the book as a whole. He tries, in *The African Witch*, to match Conrad's creation, in *Nostromo*, of a whole state alive with dissension and treachery. The Emir is senile, and the intrigues which are inevitably the prelude to succession in Africa are rife in Rimi's huge warren of a palace and the crowded compounds which line the town's deep-gullied paths. The court officials favour the Fulani claimant, Salé. His rival is the English-educated Louis Aladai, who has hurried home from Oxford to establish his claim. Aladai has the somewhat embarrassing support of his sister Elizabeth, priestess of the pagan community's most powerful juju, and of Coker, a fanatical exponent of a local brand of Christianity. The British Resident, Burwash, favours Salé and accepts his alleged nomination by the Emir. Once the successor is known, the 'palace gang' acts quickly: the Emir is poisoned, the Waziri disappears and Salé's faction takes possession of the palace. The militant opposition to this of the Aladai party is at first organized efficiently and without bloodshed by Elizabeth, as general of the 'women's war'. But it gets completely out of hand when Coker's adherents murder the missionary doctor, Schlemm. The Resident's change of heart regarding Aladai comes too late; embittered by his treatment at the hands of the English community, Aladai throws in his lot with Coker, and falls with him in the ensuing battle.

Joyce Cary's growing assurance as a writer shows itself everywhere in this story of the Rimi succession. Certain scenes etch themselves deeply on the reader's memory: the witch-trial, in which the huge, entranced figure of Elizabeth glides through the crowd to expose the witch; the market-place battle between the supporters of

Aladai and of Salé, in which Aladai is seemingly preserved from a spear-thrust by a miracle (actually by a book in his pocket); the senile Emir's nightly prowl through the hovels of his 'palace', recounting fifty-year-old battles to his favourite wife, scenting out intrigues, grumbling over broken walls and the destruction of a teapot which was a gift from Lugard; the Emir's final emergence from the looted and deserted palace by working loose the hinges of the great door and then staggering into the unnaturally silent and deserted market-place; his struggle from one barred door to another –

> At the first light of dawn the Emir had returned to the market-place, on the west side.
>
> He knocked at a door near the middle of that side. At the same time another door, further down, was opened, and a girl came out with a calabash. The door shut quickly behind her. She was dressed like a bride, but she appeared in the last stages of terror. She walked a few steps, then she fell on her knees.
>
> The Emir came up to her, took the calabash, and said, 'Thank you, my child. I was hungry.'
>
> He asked her what had happened to all the people. Had they run away? She answered, 'No, King.' But he didn't attend to her. He took the calabash, collapsed on his hams, and ate without ceremony. The girl crept away, and knocked on a door. But the door did not open. She went on creeping away, crouching almost to the ground, till she came to the main road and disappeared into it.
>
> The Emir suddenly dropped the calabash and gave a scream; jumped to his feet and ran about twenty yards, screaming; then he fell down, rolled over on his back, kicked up his little legs, and lay dead in that position, like a beetle.
>
> (p. 228)

The objectivity of this description, as of most of Cary's writing, is more apparent than real. The passage resembles a skilful film sequence which gives us the illusion that we are dispassionate onlookers while our feelings are in fact firmly engaged. Every detail conveys the Rimis' awestruck respect for their lifelong ruler and the conflict between this respect and their ritualistic compulsion to effect his death. And over and above this empathy, the reader becomes deeply involved in the political part of the novel as his feelings are manipulated by Cary's satire.

We have seen that one of the strongest misgivings expressed about indirect rule in the nineteen-thirties was that the British administrators of the system, out of a kind of romantic conservatism, but also perhaps out of a protective jealousy, preferred the picturesque traditional ruler to the Western-educated African. This prejudice had in fact been criticized by the founder of indirect rule. 'The whole attitude of the European on the Coast to the trousered Black is wrong', Lugard wrote to his wife in 1918, adding: 'One slips into it oneself in an unguarded moment';[1] indeed, the jarring jocularity of the phrase suggests he might. In *The African Witch* this prejudice is displayed at every turn by the English community who cold-shoulder Aladai, the only man who could give Rimi an honest and efficient government, and are charmed by the decadent and perverted Salé because he is 'so much of a gentleman' (p. 238). Burwash, whose name with its overtones of wishy-washy, whitewash, purr, blur and other suggestions of benign ineffectuality was a last-minute inspiration, is a kindly man whose only defects are that he sees no evil and does no good. In the finished novel this point is dramatically made in Burwash's bland refusal to believe, even after Schlemm and Aladai have rescued the mutilated Osi from Elizabeth's juju house, that witch trials are conducted in Rimi town. Needless to say, much patient questioning by the A.D.O. elicits no accusation from the terrified Osi. After this, there was no need for the explicit conversation about the Emir's powers between Aladai and his English friend Judy Coote, which occurs in the manuscript:

'But don't you understand – he is a real king in his own country. That is the whole idea – that is your English policy. The policy of Lugard. He is a much stronger king than the old Emirs before Lugard came. No one can turn him out. He has your army to keep him strong –'

'But he can't put people in prison for trifles – for nothing at all.'

'Of course, of course he can. Whenever he likes – he tells his men.

[1] M. R. Perham: *Lugard*, II, p. 604.

Karama
23.9.19

This is a picture of me crossing the Wurumu
in the dusk on a not very stout tree trunk.
It is no doubt an amusing picture, but it
wasn't at all a joke in reality. I have
crossed that d ✳✱ river 12 times now
and am getting very tired of it. There are
no crocodiles, it is true, but plenty
of mud and water. Nevertheless I enjoy
going to see my road. It is now getting
a long way into the bush. My dear,
I walked nearly 8 miles in two hours
this evening, and I am tired. Poor
fat Musa the P.A. has a very long face
of our road inspection evenings, but
he makes no attempt to keep up.

Plate V
From a letter from Joyce Cary to his wife, 23 September 1919.
Tasuki is on the right

Plate VI

Page of sketches found among the manuscript of Mister Johnson,
but possibly meant as illustrations to The African Witch

They swear lies. . . . And then perhaps they give you something in your chop, and when the Resident asks Where's the man who has a complaint, they say He's sick, and soon they say, He's dead. You don't know this country. The Resident doesn't know.'

One man who does know the country, the prevalence of its belief in witchcraft as well as the cruelty and corruption of the Emir's officials, is the missionary Schlemm. The most passionate protests against the abuses of indirect rule in the inter-war years came from the missionaries. Schlemm is partly modelled, as Cary's notes show, on Schweitzer; but he owes perhaps more to the pioneer missionary of Northern Nigeria, Walter Miller, who had the distinction of arriving in Kano in 1900 in advance of Lugard himself (he was quickly ejected), before settling down to his life's work in Zaria. Miller was fiercely critical of the British support for the Fulani Emirs whom he regarded as foreigners tyrannizing over the Hausa and pagans (in *The African Witch*, the old Emir is pagan, and the agreeable court characters Hausa: Salé is Fulani); and his report on the corruption and brutality of the Emir of Zaria, of which he had a detailed knowledge shared by no other European, was instrumental in getting that monarch deposed at long last in 1921. A lively portrait of Aliyu of Zaria is drawn in Miller's *Reflections of a Pioneer*, which was published in the same year as *The African Witch*. It is noteworthy that the real and the fictitious Emirs have the same name.

Burwash is not the only European character in the book whose ignorance of what is happening under his nose stems from a wish to keep Africans at a comfortable distance, as figures in a tropical landscape; or, as Aladai puts it in one draft, in 'a kind of native reserve with picturesque savages and religions and customs all complete'. Rackham, the commissioner of police, is in Rimi only because the job offers an open-air life and plenty of polo: the 'nicest' character in the book, Rubin, delays Schlemm with a large British breakfast when the missionary wants transport to the juju house where he knows Osi is being tortured; and the District Officer, Sangster, is 'a good pagans' man, but unlike Bewsher of Gwanki or

Bradgate of Yanrin, he had never done anything to make them richer or to develop their government. He liked the pagans, as he said, 'primitive' (p. 237). And Cary hints that the relish with which Burwash keeps repeating the slogan 'Slow but sure' also has something to do with liking people primitive. 'And then he made a little speech about the difficulty and danger of educating a primitive community in a hurry; and the great importance of inculcating character; "or guts – if Miss Coote will excuse me. I believe they are absolutely right in Katsina in their emphasis on guts" ' (p. 69). It is significant that the Education Officer's bungalow in Rimi station stands empty; even more significant, for this and other aspects of the story, that Rackham fits it up for his own amusement as a gymnasium. The anti-intellectuality of the English, their romanticism about tradition, their innate conservatism, are the factors which bring about the final holocaust, in which all parties display an admirable amount of guts and lamentably little intelligence.

It is not surprising, in view of the book's documentary vividness and its persistent satire of the British in Nigeria, that reviewers should have said *The African Witch* would 'lose all point' if Cary's request that it should not be taken as a picture of contemporary conditions in West Africa were heeded; or that they should have found that point to be 'that white interference in Africa has little result, and mostly bad.'[1]

Yet Cary's disclaimer was not disingenuous. The African setting of *The African Witch* is not the tenor but only the vehicle of what the writer has to say. The book itself is no more about indirect rule in Nigeria than *The Ancient Mariner* is about navigation in the South Seas. For when Cary spoke of the book as a work of imagination, he used the word in a Coleridgean sense. It is a book about mental life, about the fundamental passions, often driven to obsessions, which control human relationships. If he chose an African setting for such a subject, this was because, as he writes in the preface to the Carfax edition: 'Basic obsessions, which in Europe hide themselves

---

[1] *The Daily Telegraph*, 15 May 1936; *Reynold's Illustrated News*, 10 May 1936.

under all sorts of decorous scientific or theological or political
uniforms, are there seen naked in bold and dramatic action.'

2

The inner action of *The African Witch*, which is thus placed in a
setting of the Rimi succession, is a double morality. Its European
hero and its African hero are each poised between his good and his
bad angel. The European hero is the taut-nerved Irishman Rackham,
who is presented more critically than perhaps any other leading
character in Cary's works because he is a self-portrait of the writer
as he was in his early days in Nigeria, before the isolation of Borgu
had compelled him to begin thinking things out for himself. When
the book opens, Rackham is engaged to a young Oxford tutor
called Judy Coote. Small, lame, seemingly undistinguished, Judy
is gifted with intellectual vitality and so a free mind. She can be
tiresomely donnish on occasion; but her self-insight is as shrewd as
her insight into the people round her. She is Rackham's good angel,
his vital force (her tenacity of life enables her to survive at the end of
the novel), whereas Dryas Honeywood, the sister of a young
trader, who seems to enjoy the vitality of health and youth, in fact
brings Rackham near to destruction. Dryas thinks nothing out for
herself; her actions are all conditioned reflexes. On the whole the
conditioning force – an English middle-class education – has been a
morally sound one, but Dryas herself is singularly lacking in the
quality Dr Johnson termed bottom. This lack is made very explicit
in certain passages which Cary drastically cut or excised altogether
from the published novel:

> To her pictures and poetry served to elevate the mind; natural beauty
> spoke of God. To admire Nature was a religious act: but the religion
> itself was utility. Admiration of nature improved the moral muscle.
>   For all this it was quite false to say that she was a prig. There was no
> trace of self-righteousness in the girl. She was a woman of the heroic
> age, bred to be the mother of simple but real heroes. There are plenty of

her kind in the middle classes of the world, especially in the British Isles.

Her weakness, as Judy said, was the common one of all her people. Her foundations were in the mud; there was nothing solid beneath the excellent and enduring structure of her character. It would hold together; but it might sink bodily into that ancient slush on which her protestant culture floated; in common with the Rimi crocodiles.

And later on;

Rackham knew that this was his opportunity and he took it. He had seen the effect of Africa ᴏn plenty like Dryas; not women, but young men from the public schools with the same equipment as she. How well they ran on tramlines. Send them to the bush for six months and make an unexpected call; you found them clean, smart, efficient. But pull up the tramlines, the routine of business, or mining, or prospecting, and throw them into the real bush; the desert of the spirit. They were lost; they walked round in circles; they hobbled like Carthew or Prince.

They were like ships, A1 at Lloyd's, with first-class officers, but no charts. They could navigate, but they didn't know where they were, where they were going, even the shape of the seas.

Rackham himself had left school, at seventeen, in that condition. War service had not cured it. A war course at the University had only shown him that his education was not quite complete; and he had not bothered to complete it since. But he knew its limitations; and so he could see into Dryas' mind as into his own. When she said, 'Why are things so complicated?' he could have laughed at the innocence of the confusion.

Thus placed between the captive and the free, Rackham makes a disastrous choice of the captive Dryas. Aladai's choice is even more calamitous. The Irishman and the Nigerian are markedly alike. Both are highly-strung and tend to show off. The opening chapters present them both in parallel situations: Rackham, winning the race on the vicious Kraken, displays before Dryas the same kind of mastery as the mounted Aladai reveals to Judy when he quells the riot in the market-place. In one manuscript note this similarity is literally underlined: 'Aladai behaves bravely, coolly, strung up. *Just like Rackham.*' Aladai's mind, like Rackham's is a battleground between rational and irrational forces; and while two of the rational influences on his behaviour are European – Judy and Schlemm – the third, his sister Elizabeth, is African. Elizabeth is the chief priestess of the pagan juju, so that to call her rational may seem paradoxical. But Elizabeth is rational in the sense of being mistress of her fate. She does not serve the juju; she makes it serve her. Her cruelty is a means to retaining her power and does not represent a surrender of herself to irrational savagery. As a draft passage states: 'It had struck Judy that the immense confidence of the typical juju priest might be due simply to the fact he had discovered himself immune from the juju's displeasure. Elizabeth believed herself mighty because the mighty juju with which she had lived on familiar terms had never vented its jealousy upon her; or resented her carelessness and neglect.' This author's comment was rendered unnecessary by the introduction of the child Ibu, one of a number of children added in the final revision of the manuscript to supply a further set of analogies alongside those between the black and white groups of characters. Ibu, accused of withcraft, is shut up with the juju. Inured to fear by a week of terrors, including the sack of the palace, she survives and is chosen as postulant by Elizabeth who realises that, like herself, Ibu has a personality stronger than the juju. Elizabeth, like Judy, survives barbarities that would kill any other woman and her vitality is symbolized in the fact that she has no sooner recovered from the palace gang's attempt to poison her than she successfully gives birth to a child. A calm and capable commander in the women's war, she could effectively negotiate peace with Burwash and establish Aladai as Emir, were it not for Coker.

Coker is Aladai's evil genius. He does not want a bloodless war. 'His keyword was blood, but it appeared in different connexions: blood of Jesus – blood of sacrifice – blood of the wicked man – blood of the sinner – the baptism of blood' (p. 50). His maniacal preaching on the text, 'Surely the blood of your lives I will require', in the juju grove near Schlemm's mission, has had innumerable analogues all over Africa in the activities of such sects as the Watch Tower Movement, which was already rampant when Cary wrote. 'Coker's slogan was "Africa for Christ", but his conception, if you could describe his mental processes as such, was a kind of bloody sacrifice. Africa would offer herself up to Christ, in blood –

not only the blood of the whites, but her own' (p. 209). When Aladai repudiates Elizabeth's practical efforts to get him made Emir, and decides to die 'for Rimi', he destroys not only himself, but the Rimi civilization which only he could have begun to build.

The novel's dichotomy, like that of *Aissa Saved*, is thus between those who have self-confidence and those who have surrendered their self-reliance to some inner idol. Confidence, vitality, resilience are constantly displayed by the pagans and by their ruler, for whom 'there was only one world'. But it can be found too in characters ranging from Dr Schlemm, the rational Christian, to the Hausa guttersnipe, Musa. Musa is small, sickly, ignorant, and ugly; yet he is the undisputed leader of a gang of Rimi children with whom his vitality shows itself in continual play-acting and 'showing off'. This showing off is a necessary outlet for the powerful characters, and takes many forms: Musa imitating a duiker for his raga-muffins; Fanta, the Emir's favourite wife, telling stories; Ibu's exuberant chatter; the Kraken trying to throw Rackham; Tom the current 'husband' of the witch acting the European in his white suit; Rackham juggling with beer bottles; Aladai quoting Wordsworth. And the powerful man's admirers sense mastery in the hem of his garment. The child wife of Musa clutches his rag of clothing throughout their play; likewise Judy, as she follows Aladai through the hostile crowd which so surprisingly falls back before him, finds she has to overcome the impulse to cling to his coat-tail.

But the self-confidence which represents freedom is subject to many attacks. When Tom swaggers into the juju house in European dress, it is literally ripped off him by Elizabeth. Aladai's self-confidence receives as great a check when he penetrates the European juju house ('Juju for English too,' as Elizabeth remarks); he ventures into the station's Scotch Club only to find himself cold-shouldered by the members. And once again, 'where self is not, something other than self must be'. Those whose confidence has been thus impaired have to seek a new idol within. This new juju, the real African Witch of the title – for Elizabeth is not a witch, but a practical-minded priestess – is nationalism: the herd instinct of

Coker and his disciples on the one hand and on the other the identical herd instinct of Dick Honeywood, and, even more, of the stupid trader Prince: 'The word Bolshie, for example, caused one reaction – not a mental, but a nervous reaction – and the word nigger caused another. His brain did not seek to judge and know; it existed to scheme defence and satisfaction for the beasts and parasites lodged in the zoo of his character. His will was the servant of nature, the crocodile in the swamp. He had no freedom' (pp. 192-3). Other words that rouse such people to an automatic response are 'earth' and 'blood.' The name of their country can have the same effect, and their use of the feminine pronoun in speaking of it associates this response with the irrational side of their natures. One function of Judy in the book is to fight against such usages; to remind Aladai that 'Rimi' is chiefly silicates mixed with H_2O. There is a difference, she tries to show Aladai, between 'Rimi' and 'the Rimi'. The Rimi are people who are to be served with a creative energy; Rimi is an abstraction to die for only when the energy has turned to despair.

3

Joyce Cary attempts, in *The African Witch*, to do more than show the juju which every individual who despairs of himself seeks to propitiate. He goes further and tries to explore the swamp from which the crocodile arises. The key passage in the novel considered as such an exploration is Chapter XIV, which describes a boat journey down the Niger by Aladai, Judy and Dryas, on their way to visit Schlemm's mission. Generous quotation is needed to show the extraordinarily concentration of meaning in what might have been a passage of mere local colour in a lesser novelist:

> The boat was a Kakanda; built of broad planks sewn together with iron wire and caulked, apparently, with silk-cotton. It was steered by a long oar, and after tea, Dryas, feeling the need of exercise, demanded to be taught to handle this oar. She spent the rest of the evening on the poop with the helmsman.

She felt in her muscles and nerves the delight of riding and managing the power of the immense river, pouring towards the sea its thousand miles of flood. As its lift and pressure twisted the pliable craft under her, she balanced with springing knees, waiting to pull against the next gust or freshet which would send them yawing out of their course.

Judy and Aladai were chatting on the forecastle head in the shadow of the sail. She could hear them clearly except in the gusts. Their talk amused her, like the chatter of passengers overheard by an officer during a difficult crossing.

They spent an hour discussing native education; and with what excitement!

Education! On a day like this! . . .

She looked down at Judy across the waist, where the crew lay inanimate, like a heap of shining black fish in a small basket. The little woman was waving her thin hands and speaking very fast. Aladai was looking down at a girl with bandaged legs who had sat crouched against the half-deck all noon; Dryas had noticed her because she moved her place when Aladai changed his, following the shadow. . . .

It appeared that the sick girl was a witch; no, accused of it. She gazed about her like a guilty dog, hanging her head, while Judy discussed her.

'Why must Judy discuss her?' Dryas thought, angrily tugging at the oar. 'Can't she see how she feels? But Judy can't leave anything alone.'

Aladai was taking the girl to the mission, but she did not want to go. 'Then why make her?'

'Jealousy I expect,' said Judy, in a sharp, loud tone. 'That's at the bottom of most witch trials.'

Her sharp voice made Dryas smile. She thought with pity and a little contempt: 'I suppose she doesn't realise how mean it is – and how stupid. I believe Jerry is beginning to hate her. I wouldn't blame him.'

Judy and Aladai were talking about jealousy. Judy said that it was the first and worst of all vices.

'So it is,' said Dryas to herself.

It was at the root of all that was bad in everything you could think of – human relations, nationalism, religion. 'Scotch clubs,' said Aladai; but Judy hurried on in her fury against jealousy. It was the voice of the devil himself – the angel that would not stay in heaven because he could not be king of it; and it was as cunning as the Devil –

'The Rimi say that blood is jealous.'

'So it is. Creeping everywhere – into your brain and into your nerves – that's absolutely true. All the jealous gods love blood. Because jealousy

is a cannibal, feeding on itself. It would rather destroy itself than help
another.'

(pp. 155-7)

Jealousy is the topic here because the story up to this key chapter has
been a series of incidents provoked by jealousy. Jealousy, which is
in its nature self-doubt, a surrender to the irrational, has brought
these four people together on the Niger; Osi, being both pretty and
intelligent, has earned the jealousy of her co-wives whose herd-
instinct has caused them to expel her as a witch who kills babies.
But she owes her release from the juju house, like her imprisonment
there, to jealousy – the jealousy of Schlemm, who, resenting his
waning influence over his old pupil, Aladai, asks his help in rescuing
Osi. Aladai at first refuses, because of the explosive local situation;
but he is finally prevailed upon to co-operate with Schlemm.
Schlemm's determination to push home this victory leads him to
display the unscrupulousness of the really dedicated. He gets Dryas
to invite Aladai, who deeply admires her, to visit his mission.
Judy's presence is also attributable to jealousy. Twice already her
friendship with Aladai, whom she knew at Oxford, has irritated
Rackham and so provided an excuse for his interest in Dryas, whose
simple and sensuous response to life is contrasted here, as everywhere
in the book, with Judy's sharp curiosity. In inviting herself to the
mission (without knowing Dryas and Aladai to be of the party),
Judy has surrendered herself to the very form of jealousy of which
she speaks in this passage: her jealousy is a cannibal feeding on itself.
The allusion to the Devil reminds the reader that the Jehovah who
threw Satan from Heaven was a jealous god, and that there is a
jealousy of possession as well as of deprivation. Possession induces
guilt; the myth of divine sacrifice is closely linked to the concept of
a jealous god. Judy is still technically in possession of Rackham, since
she is engaged to marry him, but she knows he loves Dryas. This
knowledge has undermined her confidence and she is ready to
sacrifice herself to her own sense of guilt.

Of course, the jealousy of possession can result in acts of aggres-
sion as readily as in acts of self-immolation: the British have

connived at Aladai's expedition because their own tribal security is threatened by the presence in Rimi of an African who is better educated and more capable than most of themselves. And sometimes jealousy acts both as a destructive and a self-destructive force. This happens to Judy on the day after this voyage downstream with its talk about jealousy. The remaining member of the party, Burwash's elderly sister, Mrs Vowles, gets sunstroke. Schlemm has gone ahead to the mission; Judy accompanies Mrs Vowles back to Rimi, leaving Dryas in the care of Aladai. Afterwards she realizes that she perhaps did this to prevent Dryas returning to Rackham before her, and even, perhaps, to discredit the girl a little in the eyes of the race-conscious Rackham. Her self-scrutiny does not probe as far as the self-destructive nature of her action, which completely alienates Rackham from her. Rackham in turn surrenders to the herd-instinct of jealousy. He takes refuge in Honeywood's store and its stock of gin. The point of Rubin's characteristic pleasantry, 'When I have a drink, I feel another man and then the other man wants a drink,' becomes clear. Rackham becomes another man. Jealousy takes such complete possession of him that when the boat with Aladai and Dryas in it returns he fights Aladai and knocks him into the river. Aladai's self-confidence, earlier undermined, has been shored up by Dryas's carefully 'nice' behaviour on the return voyage; but now that he is hurled into the Niger before all his supporters and Dryas, it is sacrificed to tribal feelings. At this point the reader's mind goes back to another passage describing the voyage downstream, when night falls on the river and Aladai's attendants sing a song which he translates, line by line, for Dryas and Judy:

The spearmen broke in like a crash of trumpets; the strings shrilled like a chorus of women:

> 'Father, I am old, an old woman,
> My womb is barren, my breasts are dry,
> I cannot bear sons, I cannot feed your sons,
> They starve in the dark. The children weep for food,
> Father, accept me, take the old woman to soothe your anger
> Take me to feed them.'

The tune changed again, became slower, louder, and, as it seemed to Judy, more triumphant.

She said to Louis: 'I believe you like this song better than Schubert.'

He answered with a little impatience: 'But this is real – it is a family song. She was a real old woman – of my own blood. We are proud of her ; and I think you would be proud of her'; and then, as the spearmen broke off, he sang with the same triumphant, proud voice:

'*She threw herself into the black water.*
The river accepted the old woman.'

Then, quickening again to a dance rhythm:

'*The black water is joyful with her blood.*
It runs and leaps. It is dark and thick.
The great fish moves its tail and swims in the thick water.
He is not angry. His people remember him.
Father, my father, your children are fed.
See to the fish feast all the village crowd.
The sandbanks are full of laughing and dancing.
O father fish, many are your children.
You give amply and in abundance.
Once I was in the water and swam twisting my tail:
Now I dance with my brothers on the sandbank.'

There was a few minutes' silence after the song. Then Judy said: 'But it is worse than sad; it is terrible. And why does the father want a sacrifice?'

'I suppose he is a jealous god,' said Aladai. His voice was uncertain. He could not yet control his excited nerves.

Judy changed the subject. 'But they're not usually so sad in your Rimi.'

'They're sad now because they're poor.'

'But all people feel so now – all over the world.'

'No; white people are full of hope, because they say, "This bad time will come to an end"; or they say, "We may not beat the bad times, but our children will, and now we will fight." But these poor people do not know how to fight anything. They do not know how to fight sickness and pain and grief. They do not even know how to fight themselves.'

'And that's why you want schools?'

'Yes, to teach them to be free.'

The passage states a choice which Judy and Aladai will both have to make between self-reliance, which might enable them to fight for life, and self-immolation. Aladai is fished out of the river alive, but his confidence, which might have taught the Rimi to be free, is gone. He adopts a tragic pose, changes into native dress and tells Elizabeth that he is now determined to make war and shed his blood for Rimi. Elizabeth thinks this great nonsense and says so. When Aladai reminds her that their ancestor threw herself into the river as a sacrifice, her retort is: 'That was for good fishing and the fish came. But it won't make you chief if I get shot by some rotten Hausa with a white man's gun.' But Aladai does not listen. He is in the grip of jealousy: a jealousy of colonial dispossession which makes him send high-flown ultimatums to Burwash; a jealousy of possession which leaves him guilty at being the one Rimi in a million who has a Western education. Meanwhile, Judy has realized that she has lost Rackham to Dryas; and after her self-confidence has burnt itself out at a hilarious dinner party, she breaks the engagement and, without warning, heads for the river. This episode, so completely integrated with the theme of the book, was in fact based on an actual incident related to Cary by another District Officer on the Niger. After a slight after-dinner disagreement, the D.O.'s wife vanished. 'He found her half a mile away, heading for the river at full speed. He just took her by the arm and they walked back without a word. Neither have either of them referred to it since' (27 October 1918). In the same way, Schlemm intercepts Judy and carries her off to the Kifi mission; and desperation never again gets the better of her will to live.

But the jealous god gets his sacrifices. After Schlemm has disappeared in the attack on the mission, and Judy has taken Aladai's letter of negotiation to the Resident, Aladai is left alone with only Schlemm's books for company. Anxious and lonely, he drifts with Osi to the juju grove where Coker, armed with Schlemm's head, is preaching his gospel of sacrifice. Osi responds by throwing herself into the crocodile pool. Aladai is left partly awed and partly angered by this. He is still bemused when Dryas appears and urges him to escape, because troops are coming.

Dryas's apparent self-confidence has failed her. Cary presents her to us at the beginning of the tale as a young woman with a sedate conviction of her own superiority, a superiority of race and class, of health and youth. She is sorry for the Emir because he is old, Judy because she is lame, Aladai because he is black. But since this sense of superiority has no foundation whatever, it quickly makes way for a sense of guilt, the guilt of possession. Dryas knows she has no 'right' to Rackham, and the guilt she feels at being the cause of his hurting Judy becomes closely linked with the guilt she feels at his striking Aladai. After the fight, this guilt becomes an obsession: 'There was blood all over my dress.' Under the strain of these unwelcome experiences, the notion of service to which she has been bred gets perverted to the idea of self-sacrifice.

When Dryas walks into Coker's reach, she destroys not only herself, but Aladai as well. Judy, when she arrives on the scene to report that she has arranged a meeting between Aladai and Burwash, cannot get a hearing; Dryas insists this must be a trap: 'Look at the Indians and the Irish.' The uncertainties which give rise to hysterical nationalism have led her to embrace other people's nationalism. At this point Aladai is poised between a good and a bad angel, and he makes the fatal choice of listening to Dryas. Judy has reason on her side, but Dryas has 'character'. She is guided by the same irrational force which directs Coker's preaching and has made Osi throw herself to the crocodile; and it only remains for Aladai to join them in a final act of self-immolation to the Idol of the Tribe.

4

The African Witch is a confident, assured book, in comparison with Cary's first two novels. Its political viewpoint is a good deal more stable than that of *An American Visitor*. The reason for this is not only that Cary had himself arrived, by 1935, at a detachedly critical view of indirect rule; he had also realized that a debate on the pros and cons of colonialism is not the novelist's business, and that the reader needs to have his attention focused on the psychological grounds of race attitudes rather than on their outcome in imperial policy. 'For the fundamental question', he wrote in the Carfax Preface to *The African Witch*, 'the root of all politics, all arts, is what do men live by? What makes them tick and keeps them ticking?'

Yet for all this imaginative energy which creates a rich, complex mental life for each of the book's chief characters, *The African Witch* is for many readers, including all the African readers of it that I have met, Cary's least successful novel. A minor cause of dissatisfaction lie. in the over-neat subconscious motivation of many actions in the story. At times, the characters behave like the illustrations to a Freudian essay. Rackham, annoyed at Judy's friendliness towards Aladai, takes it out on the horse; Dick Honeywood, aggrieved because Rubin has sworn at him in the polo game, insults Aladai. Dryas's obsession with cleanliness and Judy's involuntary cattiness are other examples.

A much more serious defect of the book is implicit in its title. Cary wanted to write about the mind's fight against irrational forces, and he chose an African setting for this because the operation of such forces is particularly clear in Africa, both among Africans and among Europeans living there in small, isolated communities. But the title suggests what the book itself confirms, that the juju which masters so many characters in the story is to be thought of as a specifically African force. Cary, that is to say, confused setting and symbol when he followed Conrad in identifying Africa and the Africans with the irrational. Such symbolism, still to be found today in the romancing of a South African writer, Laurens van der Post, about the Dark Eye of Africa, is itself part of the very myth of racial superiority which Cary sought to analyse in *The African Witch*. In particular, it is responsible for much confusion in Cary's presentation of Aladai.

Aladai, we are told, has had an English school and university education. Yet he writes absurdly *babu* letters to Dryas and Burwash, treats Dryas as a being from a higher planet, and succumbs to mass hysteria at a juju ritual in which he allows Osi to sacrifice herself to the sacred crocodile. The writing of this last episode as a kind of

debate between African irrationality and European rationality is
forced in the extreme:

'We must all die,' moaned Aladai. 'He that is first – must be the sacrifice.
It is very odd all this,' said the brain in a European voice. 'I shall speak to
Miss Judy about this. Why this lust for death? It does not seem natural.
Nature wants to live—not to die. . . .'

'Rimi,' he moaned, 'Rimi, my country – I give my life – for love of
Rimi.'

'Rimi,' said the brain, 'is a *ju-ju* for the herd – the religion of the blood,
the race, the old crocodile.'

(pp. 292-3)

A passage like this does not bring Aladai to life as a man of two
worlds. It suggests, rather, that Cary failed to get his character into
focus and thus saw double. And the book's history shows us that
this is exactly what did happen. There were two nationalist heroes
about ten years apart in their conception. A bundle of papers
inscribed 'Alade and Mission Story' is all that now remains of the
story of the Black Prince which Cary attempted in the mid-twenties.
In the earliest parts of this manuscript, Aladai is not a prince, but a
clerk-interpreter – which explains the *babu* letters; and throughout
he is a hysterical character, created out of an attempt to imagine the
new nationalists of Nigeria as they appeared to the Burwashes and
Rackhams who had stayed on in the country after Cary had left.
For in the nineteen-twenties Cary still felt the administrator's
suspicion of the agitator – the 'immense black brain' which had
haunted his dreams in Borgu – and was therefore ready to explain
away nationalism in the psycho-analytical terms which were so
freely current at the period; nationalism, it was held, must be the
outcome of a sense of inferiority, and wholly irrational in its origins.

The second nationalist hero was not invented, in all probability,
until after *The African Witch* had been written. His name was actually
Isu, and he was the hero of a passion play which Joyce Cary set in the
North of Nigeria. Isu's nationalist gospel, which results in his being
handed over to the Alkali by the Governor in the role of Pilate, is
rational and humanistic; and there is nothing to suggest that on this
account it is un-African. The play which is not very good as a

play – Cary had no practical experience of the theatre – exists as a kind of amendment made to the viewpoint adopted in the novel, a viewpoint Cary was fast outgrowing, but which he half-reverted to when his agent's request for another African tale caused him to turn back to the Black Prince. In doing so, he slipped back into the old 'colonial' attitudes he was trying to satirize, and in consequence produced a novel about race prejudice which was itself prejudiced. That he was himself aware of what was happening is plain from the counter-stresses which he builds up against the view that African nationalism must be psychotic in origin: the blind prejudice of Dick Honeywood or the practical good sense of Elizabeth Aladai. But these are patently devices: Honeywood is a grotesque, and Elizabeth, with her vacillations between possession and self-possession, is never fully realized as a character (she was, in fact, a late addition to the story).

Cary's psycho-analytical approach to Dryas also belongs to the stage in his thinking represented by Aladai. The heroine of that story had accepted the friendship of the Black Prince against her natural inclinations, because she had been brought up to practice self-sacrifice and to suppress her feelings. A leading character in the earlier story is Mrs Brant, who believes in divine guidance, and whose inner voice commands her to remain in Africa among people she dislikes. Cary planned, at this stage, to call the book *The Horse's Mouth*, meaning by this the categorical imperative which is actually a projection of the individual's irrational instincts. He wrote several versions of a scene in which Mrs Brant, nearly crushed in a crowd yelling, 'Death to the whites,' revels in her situation. Mrs Brant's ghost in *The African Witch* is Mrs Vowles, who makes an unexpected and fleeting appearance in the middle of a rioting crowd, gasping, 'They'll kill us. We deserve it.' In the first reshaping of *Alade* into *The African Witch*, Mrs Vowles' masochism was much more pronounced. Dryas says to Rackham, 'Mrs Vowles was telling me that she was quite ill when she first came among the blacks. And that's why she feels so deeply about them.' In the same version, there is a much fuller account than in the published book of the motives

Plate VII

Scene on the Niger (sketch in the possession of Mrs. D. Davin)

which drive Dryas to make her last, calamitous visit to Aladai: 'She had only to ask, "What is this misery lying under all the other miseries; this solid weight which has nothing to do with heat, dirt, flies, mosquito bites, filthy greasy clothes and hair and a disgusting love affair?" and at once she knew: "It is Aladai". .... His blood was on her dress. All these blacks, how horrible they were. How she loathed them. A special kindness was owed to these people; and what had she done for them. She had wounded and deserted Aladai. She was sitting there while her fellow-whites gloated over his coming ruin.' And a later version describes this state of mind as 'something deeper than fear because it was mixed with despair; the helpless trance of a lost creature in front of a vast malignant force; irresistible, jealous'.

Once again, Cary seems to grow aware of his own prejudice as he writes about Dryas, and tries to counteract it. Judy's natural friendliness to Aladai is supposed to contrast with Dryas's strained 'special kindness'. But it does not do so because it is a relationship between tutor and pupil and so belongs to a different category of experience. Cary evades the question of simple sexual attraction between two people of different races, perhaps for the reason that at the time the novel was written this lay not only outside his observation, but also at the very perimeter of his sympathy.

In writing *An American Visitor*, Cary had found that many of his difficulties arose from the fact that his attitude to his subject matter had changed in twenty-five years. In depicting Bewsher, he had sought a way out of these difficulties by concentrating the readers' interest on the springs of his actions, on what made him tick, rather than on his political opinions. And when he came to write *The African Witch* he tried to apply the same method. But he carried with him, in his study in depth, psychological oversimplifications which were themselves dated. And there was no character in the story with sufficient vitality to resist these oversimplifications as Aissa had done. Elizabeth might have been such a character, if she had not been introduced late into the tale, and if Cary had not been in a hurry to get back to *Castle Corner*.

He was in a hurry because, in writing his first three novels, he had come to realize that in a world of rapidly changing racial attitudes he had to write about Africa in one of two ways. He could try to get imperial rule and colonial theory into historical perspective, as he set out to do in the African episodes of the *Castle Corner* trilogy; or he could find a setting in which race relations, though they existed, were free from 'period' expression and 'period' explanation. Borgu supplied such a setting. In one of Cary's last published articles, he described how three men, charged with murder and detained in the guardroom of the Kaiama barracks, insisted on him visiting them daily. 'These people had come from a village only about fifteen miles away, but they felt themselves among strangers in the town. But they looked upon me as a friend because I had been to their village, they had seen me there and knew me as a friend of their chief. They knew neither nationalism, racialism, or that sense of inferiority which underlies so much racialism and make it hysterical and psychotic' ('Joyce Cary's Last Look at His Worlds'). So Cary returns to Borgu for the setting of *Mister Johnson* in which he was to achieve the aim of every novelist by creating a world of characters who seem to exist in perfect freedom from their author.

The Terrible Boy

I

'Some day when I have a reputation and can afford to play tricks', Joyce Cary wrote to his wife in 1919, 'I shall write an enormous book, with an enormous plot. Already I have to watch myself carefully, or I grow prosy. But in this book I shall prose to my heart's content. It will be a dense book. A forest of a book, full of good timber, and bad timber, and old bogs, and swamps, and rocks, and unexpected streams, and grateful springs and frightful blasted heaths, where the bones of countless readers bleach among barren wastes' (21 November 1919). This is a good description of the trilogy of novels which was to follow *The African Witch*, but of which only the first, *Castle Corner*, was completed and published. Cary was a less accurate prophet when he added: 'I shall be damned for that book.' The reviews were, however, barely lukewarm. It was not realized that the novel was the first part of a trilogy, and accordingly reviewers complained of the story's confusing ramification from its three main branches – the Irish, English and Nigerian tales – and of the way that its characters were dismissed at the end 'with the abruptness of water run out of a bath'.[1]

The plans and sketched-out episodes of the whole trilogy, which survive in manuscript, make Cary's purposes clear, as we can see by following the course mapped for the African part of the story. *Castle Corner*'s African chapters begin with Felix Corner, the disinherited eldest son of the family, taking to the life of an Oils Rivers trader in the eighteen-nineties. This easy Trader Horn existence is soon disrupted by Felix's ambitious young nephew, Cock Jarvis, the embodiment of the new imperialism; as a member of the West

[1] Sylvia Lynd in *The News Chronicle*, 17 January 1938.

African Frontier Force, Cock Jarvis marches into the pagan kingdom of Laka across the river from his uncle's trading station and
later, when Laka is raided for slaves by the Emir of Daji to the north,
goes on to conquer Daji with a column of fifty men. Cary based
Jarvis's exploits on Lugard's 1894-5 march on Nikki, and his expedition against the Northern Emirs in 1903. The parallel with Lugard
is continued in the episodes written for the second volume, in which
Cock Jarvis returns to Daji as Resident. His Irish family hopes that he
will, on local analogies, protect their interests on the Coast; in fact,
he ruins Felix and Cleeve by the determination with which, like
Lugard, he puts down the gin trade. A scene in which Jarvis visits
the dying Emir who has become his fast friend is also very remi-
niscent of Lugard's relations with the Northern chiefs. The connexion is made even more explicit in some of Cary's notes for the
novel: 'Jarvis, much in love and disappointed in his career, goes off to
West Africa as a political officer. Here he comes at once under the
influence of Lugard's nationalist policy for the natives.' And again:
'In Africa, Cocky does battle with Killick, a direct rule man who
hopes to get rid of Lugard.'

This story gave Cary scope to develop some of the African
characters who appear in *Castle Corner*. One plan was to use the
whole manslaughter trial which Cary had presided over in Borgu in
1919, with Felix's half-caste daughter Bandy as the victim and Cock
Jarvis as the D.O. determined to protect the culprits to the limit of
his conscience because they were 'his people'. Another was to make
Cocky protest violently in Downing Street against a patrol sent to
destroy the Laka drum juju, now in the care of the sacred, handless
Azai.

We have already seen that the third volume of the trilogy was to
be largely a re-writing of the old *Cock Jarvis*, tracking Jarvis's fall
from his Edwardian position as one of the absolute rulers of the
old Empire. As one manuscript summary puts it: 'At beginning,
C.J. fierce against exploiters and also liberals, Farrant [i.e. Felix]. At
end, new theory is – exploit, develop. . . . Situation in Africa. Cocky
defending old providential régime – knocked out by zeitgeist, late.'

From all this it is clear that the century's changing ideas on colonial government were to be reflected in Jarvis's career: imperialist exploitation and conquest give place (as they did in Lugard himself) to a protective policy, exaggerated by many of Lugard's first residents into a kind of *laisser faire* and in its turn rejected by the new post-war Liberalism's concern for political and economic planning. Cary's preface to the Carfax edition of *Castle Corner* shows that the whole trilogy was to 'raise such questions as: Is there a final shape of society to be founded upon the common needs and hopes of men?' But as he there admits, a story which is first and foremost concerned with persons could not answer universal political questions. 'And in the upshot I abandoned the whole enterprise, and turned to write about the simplest of characters in a simple background, with the simplest of themes, Mister Johnson, the artist of his own joyful tale.'

Mister Johnson, the best of Cary's African novels and considered by many people (including at one time its author) to be his best novel, would not be as good as it is were it not built on the ruins of the *Castle Corner* trilogy. True, it makes practically no use of the old stone; though the songs Cary wrote for Jingler, the African wandering minstrel, offered good practice for Johnson's songs. But *Castle Corner* and its roughed-out sequels gave Cary the chance to work out two seams in his writing which were not fruitful to him as a novelist: a seam of political theorizing which, as he realized, was not really the novelist's concern; and a seam of Old Coaster yarns which sometimes mar the earlier novels with meaningless horror and violence. Another circumstance helped. During the writing of *Mister Johnson*, Cary was asked by the Liberal Party Committee to write a book for their Book Club; and this work, *Power in Man*, published two months before *Mister Johnson*, channelled off Cary's political theories into rigorously abstract writing. *Mister Johnson* was in consequence an unadulterated work of art; and Cary's words quoted above imply that he was helped to make it so by the fact that it is a book about an artist.

2

Mister Johnson, like almost every masterpiece, has been mis-understood from the day of its publication. Its African setting is largely responsible. With *The African Witch* fresh in their memories, reviewers decided to treat the new novel as a portrayal of the Negro mind, whatever that abstraction may be. A *Times Literary Supplement* comment is typical: 'Mr Cary has personified the maladjustment of races and civilizations in "Mr Johnson".' And the mid-century's obsession with race relations still distorts the book for black and white readers alike. One African admirer of Joyce Cary classes the work (though with his tongue a little in his cheek) among those European novels that have to end by either shooting or hanging the African hero because the writer doesn't know what else to do with him,[1] and I have heard sensitive English readers protest that *Mister Johnson* is a 'patronizing' book, since Rudbeck's feelings for Johnson correspond to those of a man for a favourite dog that he is compelled to shoot.

The best approach towards a refutation of such ideas about the novel is through a study of Johnson's evolution in Cary's mind. As the Carfax preface shows, Johnson began as an amalgam of two clerks Cary had known in Nigeria: the clerk at Nafada who wrote home thrilling and totally untrue accounts of the war, and Mr Graves in Borgu, who, for all his inexperience as a clerk, did such surprising things as sitting up all night copying a report in order that Cary should not get into trouble. A notebook which probably dates from the late twenties show that these two real men had already been fused by Cary into a figure for one of his projected sketches of African life:

Mr. Montague, devoted – his letters home – his prayers – his row with

[1] Davidson Nicol: *On not being a West African*, Ibadan University Press, 1953.

the town—his pluck, his devotion—up all night writing reports. His tears when reproached about the Germans.

(N63)

Later, Johnson grew into the hero of several putative novels. One of them appears to end with Johnson materially prosperous but morally ruined:

> The book then is the study of a human soul gradually giving way to a crime – showing how it happens, from uncertainty, from ignorance of self. Johnson doesn't know till the end whether he's very wicked or very clever.
>
> General idea. That he ought to be taught what is true and right, about the nature of himself and the world. What is good (that gives liberty) what is bad, that restricts it.

(N73)

An alternative scheme, possibly later than the above since it appears to end as the book does, gives much fuller treatment than the final novel to Johnson's marital troubles, and in so doing presents him as a man of two worlds 'lost between two civilizations'.

Both these last two schemes failed to satisfy Cary, because both were stories of failure. Johnson the juvenile delinquent and Johnson the *demi-evolué* were each implicitly contrasted with some ideal Johnson; in one case a properly educated man, and in the other an unspoilt child of nature. There was, however, nothing inadequate about the Johnson who was taking shape in Cary's imagination and was soon to replace these other shadowy personages. Mister Johnson is one of those rare literary figures who take possession of their creator; and Cary ensures that he shall take possession of us in exactly the same way.

This becomes clear if we look at the linear development of the novel. At first sight it appears to consist of a series of sharply defined rises and falls in Mister Johnson's fortunes: from his first triumph as Rudbeck's right hand man, and escort to Mrs Rudbeck, to his dismissal by Tring who is outraged to discover that the road money has been taken without authority from the cash tank; from enjoying the confidences (though not the confidence) of Sergeant Gollup, at whose store he manages to get the job of clerk,

to a further dismissal; from his creation of the Fada road in collabora-
tion with the returned Rudbeck, to a third sacking when Rudbeck
discovers that beer for the roadgangs has been obtained by means
of an illegal levy on lodgers in the zungo; from the magnificent
parties he throws in the zungo on money and drink stolen from
Gollup's store, to his arrest and death subsequent on his murder of
Gollup. Johnson's own violent changes of mood seem to conform
to this pattern. When he is up, he is up:

> Out of the way, fool chile; when Johnson go walkum
> De whole worl' make path for him, all same for de lions of de forest
> De whole sea go dry for him all same dat King Moses from Egypt.
>
> (p. 135)

and when he is down, he is down:

> 'Oh Gawd! O Jesus! I done finish – I finish now – Mister Johnson done
> finish. . . . Why you so big bloody dam' fool, you Johnson?'
>
> (p. 20)

But in fact this pattern of pride going before a fall only represents
Johnson as he is seen from one point of view, which is certainly not
the author's. We might call it Ajali's viewpoint. Ajali, it will be
remembered, is the stores clerk burdened with an exaggerated
sense of justice who waits in delighted expectation to see Johnson's
follies lead him to a bad end. Because Cary himself began by shaking
his head over Johnson he takes a certain mischievous pleasure in
making us, the readers, shake our heads in a similar manner before
the real force of Johnson's character turns over, like a tornado,
this superficial view of him. When Cary speaks of Johnson as the
artist of his own joyful tale he means, I think, that Johnson was able
to transform a story of failure, in Cary's mind, into a triumph;
and this is just what Cary makes him do in the book. Johnson is
never down for long before being carried up to the crest of his own
vitality. Two minutes after his despair at finding a crowd of his
creditors waiting to complain to the District Officer, Blore, he is in
ecstasy at the beauty of his own handwriting: 'The thickening of the
stroke as it turns over the small loop makes a sensation. He feels it
like a jump of joy inside him. But the grand sweep, the smooth,

powerful broadening of the lower stroke is almost too rich to be borne. He gives a hop in his chair, coming down hard on his bottom, laughs, puts his head on one side and licks his lips as if he is tasting a good thing' (p. 21). And later on, when Johnson has lost his government job and can get nothing better than two pounds a month with the Cockney storekeeper, Gollup, who kicks and beats his clerks, he 'gets a grip of the new situation by creating a glory of it' – to quote a manuscript note; the glory being the fantasies of England, home, and beauty which he and Gollup pursue together in their Sunday afternoon drinking bouts. From the worst disaster so far, his dismissal by Rudbeck after the road is finished, Johnson recovers by another creative act, the splendid eloquence of his indignation against Rudbeck. And the treachery of his old friend, the Waziri, is turned into a stirring (and completely untrue) tale of Johnson's victory over the Waziri's thugs, a tale which travels as far as Tripoli and Khartoum.

The artist's extraordinary resilience, which Cary was to make the subject of *The Horse's Mouth*, shows itself in the way Johnson spends some of his happiest moments in the guardroom before and after the trial, in the company of policemen. Like Johnson, the policemen live in the moment; their mood is that of 'the everlasting camp, of pilgrimage'. But whereas they pass the hot hours away in a state of contented vacancy, singing the same old songs and grumbling over the same old grudges, Johnson's vitality compels him to turn the happiness of these times into a new song. For the justification of Cary's use of the present tense throughout the book is not so much that Johnson lives in the moment as that he lives the moment. 'To him Africa is simply perpetual experience, exciting, amusing, alarming or delightful, which he soaks into himself through all his five senses at once, and produces again in the form of reflections, comments, songs, jokes, all in the pure Johnsonian form' (p. 92). Johnson's method of filing, which reduces Rudbeck to gibbering profanity, is the work of an artist who seeks to connect the fragments of experience into a story.

Usually the hero of Johnson's inventions is Johnson himself, whether the invention is an artifact, like the Drum Song, or an act, such as his lordly refusal to betray confidential reports to the Waziri:

> 'It is nice to get presents,' Johnson says, smiling and looking round the group. He does not know what he is going to do yet. At the moment he is the centre of interest. He has an audience. It is waiting to follow him and his deeds. The situation has been given into his hands like wood to be carved or a song to be sung.

(p. 34)

But though Johnson is the hero of his own inventions, his daydreams are far from the paranoic's delusions of greatness. His triumphs have centrifugal force; when he slips into Rudbeck's office in his absence and gives the messengers the day off, they are well aware of the complex motives of good nature and glory which prompt this action. So in the native jail, and seemingly at the end of his resources, he gives away to Saleh his last proud possession, his English shoes, out of the same motives of glory and good nature. For Johnson's vitality is not only creative but generous as well. He is by nature Friday's child, loving and giving. 'He gives friendship but he has no time to ask whether he gets it.' In fact, like most of Cary's expansive characters, he gets treachery in return for friendship. He is one of those destined to 'go love without the help of anything on earth'.

Johnson, as Rudbeck says, has jump; a creative quality which is thrown into relief by the boredom of other characters, notably Ajali and Rudbeck's wife, Celia. Ajali is introduced with a potent image:

> Cut off at the waist by the counter, on which he rests his fingers, he seems to lurk in the hot, stinking twilight of the shed like a scorpion in a crack, ready to spring on some prey. But Ajali does not move at all and his insect face wears a most human expression of boredom.

(pp. 15-16)

The follies of Johnson are the one thing that can rouse Ajali; but whereas Johnson can inspire in most people a genuine and generous delight, all he can produce in Ajali is the perverted, ingrowing creativity of *Schadenfreude*: Ajali, gloating over Johnson's exploits, is 'a kind of poet', but the kind who has to belittle and smear. He is one of those beings 'wasted by boredom and loneliness and selfishness until they have become a new kind of creature, a sort of sub-humanity which can smile and eat and live at a level of corruption and misery which would kill a real human being in a day or two' (p. 126). Johnson likes Ajali's company because he likes an audience; but he rightly resents Ajali's belittlement of his visions: 'How anyone tell stink bug about de glory of God?'

For a time Celia is in grave danger of becoming as sub-human as Ajali. Like Dryas Honeywood, she is the product of a middle-class education which has given her no more specific preparation for marriage than a vague sense of duty. A District Officer's wife, she knows, must take a helpful interest in her husband's work. But Rudbeck, absorbed in his road, doesn't need her interest; so Celia has nothing to do in Fada except stare at the landscape in the vague, generalizing manner of a young woman brought up to find foreign countries fascinating and picturesque. Her vision is sharply contrasted with Johnson's way of seizing upon the uniqueness of things, his 'articulation of minute particulars' to use a phrase of Blake's. 'But to Celia Africa is simply a number of disconnected events which have no meaning for her at all. She gazes at the pot-maker without seeing that she has one leg shorter than the other, that she is in the first stages of leprosy, that her pot is bulging on one side. She doesn't really see either woman or pot, but only a scene in Africa' (pp. 92–93). Johnson is also an abstraction to her. She privately calls him Wog, because for her he is not an individual, but only the typical comic black, 'a perfect quaint'. And because to her one African is as like another African as one pot is like another pot, Fada begins to pall. She has nothing to do there; nothing to create. But her will to make a life persists. She must make something, so in the end she makes scenes.

Throughout Celia's first stay in Nigeria she is contrasted with Johnson's wife, the 'bush' girl, Bamu. Like all African girls, Bamu has been educated for marriage, and calmly and sensibly slips into her new role, 'humming to herself like a bee in a box'. In spite of this, the Johnson household runs into quite as many difficulties as the Rudbeck one; but whereas Celia becomes neurotic because she is ignored by an independent young husband, who does not need her help, Bamu suffers from the care Johnson lavishes upon her in his wish to make her a proper Government wife. To her this is all foreign nonsense, and the fact that Johnson is a Southern stranger means that her relationship with him is a dutiful one, but not lasting; like many African women, she feels that she still belongs to her father's household. So that while Bamu starts with an advantage over Celia, in that she understands her new role and is contented with it, the Johnson marriage ends in treachery; whereas the Rudbecks' persists in contented adjustment. This is only made possible by Celia returning pregnant for the Rudbeck's second tour in Fada. For now she begins, both figuratively and literally, to make a new life. In this new role she starts to behave exactly like Bamu. Both wives are indifferent to their husbands' activities on the new road; both patiently uproot themselves and carefully repack their household goods whenever the ups and downs of their husbands' careers require them to do so.

Celia was a rather unpleasant character in some early versions of the story. One idea had been to make her responsible for Johnson's dismissal after the completion of the road. But because Johnson himself took increasingly imaginative control during the writing of the novel, characters such as Celia began to take their colouring from Johnson's good nature. Blore had originally been Celia's father, and a chilly, repressive force; in the published novel he has faded away as if dissolved by Johnson's exuberance, which he finds so alarming. Another version made Bulteel an incompetent and unco-operative Resident, instead of the genial father figure of the novel who enjoys outwitting the Treasury for the sake of Rudbeck's new road. Saleh also, who threatens to be as nasty a character as Salé in *The African Witch*, is given his moment of creativity, though it is admittedly of a narcissistic kind: 'moving about the room in order to feel the beauty of his movement and the delight of his life' (p. 76). Even Tring – 'a rat but a clean honest rat' as Cary calls him in a notebook (73N) – has something to make; the career of Governor-General Tring, K.C.M.G.; while the brutal Gollup 'is creator too – self-satisfied, happy – master of his store' (MS.). And Johnson's slavey, the devoted Sozy, was added quite late in the story's composition, to show that we must go on creating our role in the world until we die. As Cary wrote to Mark Schorer: 'In this book the problems of Rudbeck *making* his road, his wife *creating* her independent life (as she must do for his happiness as well as hers) Johnson creating his personal legend and the careerist making his career – all immersed in the world of creation – of free imagination – of injustice, of change – are those of actual souls faced with personal problems which are also universal ones.'

3

The centre of interest in *Mister Johnson* is not, however, the relationship of the married couples, but the relationship between Johnson and Rudbeck. In many ways this is an extension of what Conrad attempted in his short story, *The Secret Sharer*, in which a man in authority takes the most inexplicable risks with his ship and his own career in order to let a fugitive escape from conventional justice. The deep underlying affinity between Conrad's two men is expressed in their physical resemblance; in *Mister Johnson* the same thing is indicated in similarities of temperament. 'Rudbeck, like Johnson, has the power of refusing to notice unpleasant things until they force themselves upon him. This gives him much happiness and many sudden depressions' (p. 78).

This sense of identity had been experienced by Cary himself during his closing months in Borgu, when he and Mr Graves had in common that they were the only men of Western education in a vast lonely tract of bush. Cary made a joke of this feeling in his letters, but it was very real at the time. 'The world of a clerk is strange. Here he is as much a foreigner as I am', he writes in August 1919. When Mr Graves tidies his office table, Cary has to tidy his.

And on 2 September he writes: 'I've found out Graves' chief fault. Like me – as you said once – he thinks he knows everything.' But the sedate Mr Graves was in fact very unlike the inventive Johnson. For in the novel the great bond between the clerk and the administrator is their common delight in making something; especially in the creation of the great Fada road.

It is important to notice that the real creative force always emanates from Johnson. As one sketch for the plot put it: 'Johnson is creative stream, inspiring the creators, and angering fools, the duds, the *stuck*. . . . The man inspired – i.e. Rudbeck and the road. Johnson shows him how to do it – gets the men, etc.' (N73). Cary states several times in *Mister Johnson* that Rudbeck was born to receive inspiration rather than to give it. 'He doesn't change his mind easily after he, or somebody else, has made it up for him' (p. 46); 'Rudbeck himself has jump, though only for the one game; the one idea *that has been given him*, the Fada road' (p. 83). He absorbs ideas from Johnson without realizing their source. It is Johnson who first gives him the idea of keeping the road work going by drawing on the cash tank in anticipation of next year's vote; Johnson who finds the beer to make the pagans contented on the road's most northerly stretches. Tasuki, the road foreman of Cary's pioneering days in Borgu, appears under his own name in the novel, but is deliberately kept as flat a character as possible in order that no one shall steal Johnson's thunder – or, as Cary puts it in describing the completion of the road, his power and glory.

These chapters dealing with the way the road gets finished are the most vigorously written in the book, because they recapture a triple excitement. First, there is the excitement of Tasuki and the road gangs, a simple pleasure in seeing the road appear, such as Cary had experienced in Borgu when he built his first road during the dry season of 1919-20: the pleasure of surveying the route, of beating the big drum to call in the village gangs, and of watching the road grow and plunge into the hitherto unopened bush. 'I cannot explain the pleasure of seeing a road which one has planned and surveyed in actual being, but it is a very unusually keen pleasure'

(9 September 1919). And even in 1919 Cary felt, as we have seen, a deeper pleasure than this: the satisfaction of knowing that he was opening Borgu for trade. But as far as Rudbeck is Cary's 1919 self he does not look further than an increase in the district's revenue when he weighs up the effects the road is likely to produce. The third and strongest excitement is that which was growing in Cary's mind and the minds of many other Africanists of the nineteen-thirties at the thought of the continent's economic liberation. The old protect-ive view – that held, for example by Blore, who thinks roads and railways have ruined the old Nigeria – is associated with the senti-mental feelings of Celia, for whom the squalor and misery of Fada are picturesque. For Cary himself, Fada is a slum of the spirit:

> Poverty and ignorance, the absolute government of jealous savages, conservative as only the savage can be, have kept it at the first frontier of civilisation. Its people would not know the change if time jumped back fifty thousand years. They live like mice or rats in a palace floor; all the magnificence and variety of the arts, the learning and the battles of civilization go on over their heads and they do not even imagine them.

(p. 99)

So the final excitement of Cary's description comes from a belief in the liberation which the road is to bring. The description of the road's opening accordingly has the force of a vision, Cary's own vision of the twentieth century breaking into Borgu. For the pagans swinging their hoes on the last stretch, the road is an object of pride; something to sing about. But they are ignorant of its real function. Then they hear in the distance a noise 'between drumming and gun-fire'. The terms are exact, because the road is a promise and a threat; it will bring to Fada both the blessings and the curses of civilization. Some of the roadmen run away from this liberation; the rest stand their ground to greet with cheers the first lorry to drive over the Fada road.

Rudbeck does not cheer. 'Rudbeck, with a puzzled, disconcerted expression, rides away to find Tasuki: he had not realized, perhaps, that the road would open itself.' He not only feels the lassitude and irritability of the artist whose picture or poem is finished, but he must face all the social problems the new road has brought. For Johnson's inspiration has not only given Rudbeck the liberating happiness of making something; it has also freed his mind by compelling him to look beyond his immediate tasks in Fada and ask himself what he is doing there. A man of naturally short views, Rudbeck is forced by the drive of Johnson's visions to take long ones. And this further liberation is a painful birth. Full of misgivings at his own achievement, Rudbeck is outraged at the unorthodox methods which have made the completion of the road possible. He is ready to punish, in Johnson, his own temerity; and Johnson is once more dismissed.

The injustice of this is glaring to the reader. Apart from some confusion over what belongs to him personally and what belongs to the road fund, Johnson's methods of getting beer for the road gangs have been no more reprehensible than the ways Rudbeck found for financing the road during his previous tour. Accordingly, when Johnson after this last dismissal goes entirely to the bad, kills Gollup in the course of a robbery and is condemned to death, Rudbeck is burdened with a sense of guilt. This guilt is an important theme in the novel. It has even stronger grounds in earlier versions of the tale. In these, Rudbeck's failure to understand and appreciate Johnson was illustrated by Cary's handling of an incident of his Borgu days. Johnson sat up all night to finish a report for Rudbeck, who tossed it into the tray without a 'thank you', and then accused his haggard clerk of having been up all night taking part in the banned *bori* dancing. Johnson's departure at the completion of the road was also brought about in a way which reflected even more adversely on Rudbeck than does the printed form of the episode. In the early version, the road was opened by two rather dreadful young Englishmen driving from Morocco to the Cape. After an evening spent telling Rudbeck how to do his job, they depart with a hint that Johnson is too attentive to Celia; and Rudbeck, seeing that Johnson is watching (with innocent delight) Celia at her swim, literally kicks him out. This scene was wrong for a number of reasons (in particular, a simpler symbol was needed for the invading twentieth century), but it suggests that the unimaginativeness of Rudbeck's behaviour towards Johnson was an important element in the story right from the start.

I think there is an autobiographical origin to this part of the tale. *Mister Johnson* is dedicated 'To Musa', and one of the sets of notes which Cary made has among its list of events which might be used: 'Row about the umbrella. Ilesha. Red Head's indignation.' This harks back to an incident which took place in August 1919, at the time Cary was building his road and initiating Mr Graves into his duties. At the time he described the affair as 'a grand row about a dashed old brolly'. What happened was that Musa, the Political Agent, somehow or other got the Chief of Ilesha entitlement to a state umbrella. Presumably the transaction involved a tidy sum. Cary's indignation over Musa's corruption was quite as fierce as that of Rudbeck when he finds Johnson has been taking a road-toll. But when Musa's trial took place two months later Cary (who had influenza) was in much the same state of dejection as Rudbeck is in when he is compelled to try Johnson:

> We were a strange party. I sat behind my enormous table with the patient air of the man who can't raise his voice because it hurts him; Musa sweated, literally poured with sweat, in his indignation and outraged virtue; the Chief of Ilesha, a witness said to have been bribed by Musa, who is over six feet high, of frightful emaciation, and hideous cold protruding eye, with every line of his debauched countenance speaking his guile, treachery and folly, fluted in a high voice one contradiction after another, the mallam rolled his white eye in the background with a look of concentrated malice and venom difficult to imagine, and the Emir in the middle sat unmoved and calm, and probably half asleep.

(4 November 1919)

The trial ended inconclusively. Musa got off for lack of evidence. That Cary afterwards came to regret this fruitless interference with the private world of his faithful and (on the whole) competent Political Agent is suggested not only by the dedication of *Mister Johnson* to Musa with the affectionate quotation 'Remembered goodness is a benediction', but also by a short story called 'Adamu' written in the nineteen-thirties, and probably not long before

Mister Johnson. In this the short-tempered young Assistant District Officer of Fada, who is exactly like Rudbeck, finds that his office messengers, including the venerable old Hausa Adamu, have been taking bribes. Adamu is charged and is on the point of being sentenced when the A.D.O. is called away to the clerk's office next door. While he is there another European walks in to ask if he can cash a cheque. They talk about the messenger, and the stranger, who has been years in the country, throws new light on Adamu's behaviour by his lenient view of 'dashes'. The A.D.O. returns to dismiss the case, and leaves the court in a state of inner confusion:

> The A.D.O. hurried away on foot, without waiting for his pony. He felt confused, ashamed. But above all, he felt a kind of panic at the nearness of his escape. He knew now that Adamu was probably a better man than himself, in fact, he had always known it. He had always respected the old man. He knew that he was the honoured father and godfather of the family household, and yet he had nearly wrecked and broken that honest good life. Only a pure stroke of luck, two or three strokes of luck, the second wire, the visit of White, and White's own sudden impulse wherever it came from, to give him a sidelight on native ideas. . . .

'Adamu', which incidentally has a lot to say about the eccentric filing system of the clerk, Mr Montague, is a bridge between the case of Rex *v.* Musa and *Mister Johnson*; Cary even makes use, in its few pages, of the kind of parallel he extends all through the novel, by hinting that Adamu's bribe-taking is just as much a social convention as is the A.D.O.'s readiness to risk Government money in cashing a substantial cheque for an unknown white man.

Musa was not, of course, such a paragon as Adamu. 'Not so lazy as he was' is the limit of Cary's praise of him in his Borgu handing-over notes. Adamu is an unconvincingly virtuous character because the short story is written out of a sense of guilt. *Mister Johnson*, by contrast, is a story about a liberation from guilt, and the increasingly sympathetic presentation of Rudbeck during the story's evolution in manuscript suggests that Johnson, as he became increasingly 'real' to Cary, performed something of the same function for his creator. Racial superiority and racial guilt both represent a failure of the imagination, an inability to see people as people and not symbols. 'If you make Johnson into a symbol he will become a phoney', Cary wrote to the American adaptor of *Mister Johnson* for the stage. Yet reviewers and critics (and illustrators) have repeatedly seen Johnson as a racial symbol and in so doing have revealed that the novel's climax has been lost on them.[1]

Until this climax, Rudbeck never succeeds in seeing Johnson as a person. He comes near to doing so at one point, but the notion eludes him. 'Mr. Sturdy passing through shows Rudbeck that Johnson is a good man', reads a manuscript note. In the published book this becomes the half-perception of Rudbeck himself when Bulteel comes to inspect the first fifty miles of road:

> 'He's the man with the ideas,' Rudbeck says. Then, staring at Johnson under his long lock which droops over his right eye, he says in a tone of gratified surprise, 'In fact, if it wasn't for him and Tasuki there wouldn't be a road even up this far.'
>
> Bulteel chuckles and says politely, 'Yes, yes, I've heard of your excellent work, Mr – ah – Johnson.' He doesn't believe that anyone does excellent work. But Rudbeck is still surprised by his own remark. He gazes at Johnson thoughtfully, as if trying to get a new conception of him. Then he gives a snort of laughter, which means that the accepted idea will have to do for the present, and says, 'He keeps us all merry and bright.'
>
> (p. 150)

When Rudbeck is in this genial mood, his view of Johnson is not very different from Celia's when she calls him 'Wog'; he is the real quaint, a sort of attendant nigger minstrel. When he is depressed, as he is once the road is finished and a crime wave for which he is called to account sweeps through Fada, his view of Johnson reverts to the equally racial simplication given him by Blore: 'the worst type – probably dangerous too – a complete imbecile, but quite capable of robbing the safe'. This of course is Tring's view, and is well represented in a book on Nigeria written only three years before *Mister Johnson* was published, which actually uses the term

[1] A striking recent example: '[Mrs Dunnett] believed, and stated, that Africans were not, and would never be, able to govern themselves. Joyce Cary's *Mr Johnson* told you, in her view, all you needed to know.' Conor Cruise O'Brien: *To Katanga and Back*, p. 108.

'Wogs' and describes them as 'a hoard of quasi-literates, parasitic, litigious, showy, noisy, insolent and as irresponsible as they are untrustworthy. They wear the white man's clothing, speak pidgin English, and, by writing petitions on anonymous charges, can create an activity in Government circles that is as mischievous as it is ridiculous.'[1]

One attempt to challenge this racial simplication is made through Benjamin, the post office clerk. He is the sort of character produced in every racialist argument: the sober, seemingly reliable man who suddenly, and to his own surprise as much as everybody else's, steals from his employer. Cary manages, with great economy of means, to suggest that this instability has nothing to do with race, but depends on psychological factors which operate in any society. In fact he was to go on to a full treatment of this type of character in Sara of *Herself Surprised*. He cannot, however, give much room in *Mister Johnson* to Benjamin, since the story must focus on Rudbeck's liberation from the view of Johnson as Wog.

This happens after the trial. That he should have to try Johnson is regarded by the embittered Rudbeck as just one more example of the bad luck which has begun to dog him. Full of a sense of guilt towards Johnson, and of the resentment which guilt breeds, he sinks into self-pity. It is interesting that in one draft of the novel Cary describes Rudbeck's state of mind by means of the image he was to use in his next novel to describe how imaginative vitality is crushed in the delinquent boy, Charley. Although adult officialdom is patient and even kind with Charley, it stifles him by an imposed sense of guilt. As he gets into the police car at the end of the book –

> He feels his arm gripped and he is pushed head first under the hood into an opening so small, dark and narrow that he is sure it can never contain him. 'They'll smother me' is the first thought that occurs to him for some minutes. But he submits, patiently and humbly, to be pushed.

So Rudbeck's submission to a shrunken life, to the orders of 'Them', is described in one draft of the closing chapters of *Mister Johnson*:

[1] W. R. Crocker: op. cit., p. 207.

It seems to his feelings that he has had a great loss or grief . . . he continues
to feel, especially when he is not thinking about anything definite, as if
life has become smaller, narrower; as if some fate has closed upon him,
like a box. He thinks he is suffering from some unique and mysterious
neurosis.

(cf. p. 224 of the novel)

What is striking here is that the similarity is between Rudbeck and
the delinquent Charley; not between Charley and the equally
delinquent Johnson. At the trial, it is Rudbeck, the judge, who is
captive and the prisoner Johnson who is free. The image first used
of Rudbeck and then saved up for Charley is of a mental captivity
such as Blake often describes, consequent upon the exile or rejection
of the imagination. Without Johnson, Rudbeck shrinks to an
administrative robot. He no longer builds roads in defiance of
Treasury stinginess. On the contrary, he is ready to be pushed, to
do anything the Secretariat requires of him; even to hang Johnson.

In the end Johnson, free himself, once again sets Rudbeck free.
Johnson is Blake's Orc, who always breaks loose because he is the
heart which cannot stop beating, creative vitality itself:

Soon as she saw the terrible boy, then burst the virgin cry:

I know thee, I have found thee, and I will not let thee go:
Thou art the image of God who dwells in darkness of Africa,
And thou art fallen to give me life in regions of dark death.

This liberation comes, as it always comes in Blake's myth, when
Rudbeck sees Johnson as a person and not as the entertaining or unreliable native. It begins when, a few minutes after Rudbeck has
attempted to follow official instructions and treat Johnson completely as an *object*, by weighing him, Johnson suddenly suggests
Rudbeck should shoot him instead. It is completed when Rudbeck
acts on this suggestion. With a very sure artistic instinct, Cary
omitted from the final version an account of the thoughts which
lead Rudbeck to shoot Johnson. The passage is over-explicit, but it
is worth quotation because it confirms what I have said about
Cary's intention in the closing pages of the novel – and unless this
intention is grasped the tale becomes mere melodrama:

All at once, Rudbeck is aware of himself and Johnson as they really are. He sees them isolated and real in the silence. He sees himself sitting in his chair, aloof and official, in the attitude of a mock official devotion. He feels with overwhelming force Johnson's living reality: his agony, his courage.

He feels inexpressibly mean and contemptible. His correct attitude, his neat sympathy appear what they are, part of a game or technique used to protect him from the need of real action, real responsibility. 'But what can I do,' he asks himself, 'I've got my orders.'

The answer springs at him as if from the air.

'You know perfectly well what you ought to do. There's no doubt this time – the only question is, are you going to funk it.'

He puts it away promptly.

The very idea of killing Johnson with his own hands is horrible to him and besides, as he admonishes himself 'Damn it, the whole country would know about it – I don't want to get kicked out of the service.'

But at once the thought jumps back into his mind like a living presence. 'You know what's right this time – are you going to funk it.'

Rudbeck gets up quietly. . . .

The writing of this passage is awkward and stilted, much as a monologue would sound if it occurred in the middle of a strictly realistic play. This is because in the novel as finally written we are so closely identified with Rudbeck that our illusion would be broken if we were told what he was thinking. All we need is to be aware of Johnson himself and so experience the imaginative liberation which moves Rudbeck to action: the realization that Johnson is not absurd, or dangerous, or pathetic, but that he is, as the top of each page reminds us, *Mister* Johnson—gifted with the mastery to shape his own life and even to shape its close.

In the manuscript of *Mister Johnson* as it went to the printer, Rudbeck was still, at the end of the book, confused and puzzled by what he had done. Cary found the right ending only at the last minute. It is an ending which shows the old relationship restored, so that Johnson is once again the inspirer, and Rudbeck the inspired, the man set free to act freely: 'But Rudbeck, growing ever more free in the inspiration which seems already his own idea, answers obstinately, "I couldn't let anyone else do it, could I?" '

The Comedy of Freedom

Joyce Cary's years in Africa were cut off from the rest of his life. Although he spent two long leaves in England, his marriage and the war separated these periods from his pre-war existence; and the fact that he was not allowed to take his wife with him to Borgu made the break between his life in Nigeria and his subsequent career in England a marked one. After his return in 1920, he lost touch almost completely with his former colleagues of the Nigerian political service. His only other visit to Africa was in 1943, four years after he had published the last of his 'African' novels.

This isolation of his life in Africa from what went before and after it was all to Cary's advantage as a novelist. It gave a peculiar sharpness and clarity to his recollection of events; recollections which he could at any time confirm by looking up his journal-letters. He thus had under his hand, when he began to write stories about Africa, a body of experience which was as distinct and close-textured as a sculptor's block. At the same time the remoteness of Africa, both from his readers and, after a few years, from Cary himself, gave him complete freedom to hew the block into whatever shape he pleased. I do not mean that Cary profited from his readers' unfamiliarity with his setting to tell Old Coaster stories (although he did do this sometimes), but that the African setting enabled him to achieve 'aesthetic distance' and so create a world apart. The creation of such a world, immediately recognizable to the reader so that he carries his awareness of it into ordinary life and says, 'What a Jamesian episode' or 'That was a Compton-Burnett evening,' is a high achievement for the novelist. Cary found it much easier to make such a world out of his African experiences, which were finite and distanced, than out of the flux of English life to which he had returned.

Because it is a world apart, Joyce Cary's Africa, though it may often give a shock of delighted recognition to the reader who knows Nigeria, is Joyce Cary's Africa and no one else's. It certainly is not the Nigeria of 1915 or 1936 as it might be recalled by the average expatriate of either date. Still less is it a Nigerian's Nigeria, though this is often held against Cary by African readers who believe that Dicken's London and Hardy's Wessex 'really' existed. The fact is that Cary resembled these writers, and every other serious novelist, in possessing an imagination which 'dissolves, diffuses, dissipates, in order to recreate'; and the world of his re-creation has a poetic intensity which makes it most unrealistically real.

Joyce Cary's manuscripts reveal this imagination in the act, tirelessly at work to achieve that kind of creation in which, to use his own words: 'each note has to count and it must not be superfluous'. Many examples of this economy have been given in the previous pages, and others can be found by opening Cary's early novels at any page – say the first page of the first novel, *Aissa Saved*, where the three opening sentences tell us that Shibi Rest Camp on the Niger was built by Bradgate; that he was not allowed to use it as his station on account of the mosquito-ridden swamp behind it; and that later it was turned over to a mission. There is a good deal more here than mere scene-setting. It is characteristic of Bradgate, who never sees what is happening under his nose, to overlook the swamp, and equally characteristic of the missionaries to look beyond it to things not of this world. For the anopheles mosquito, capable of killing two million people a year, is a living proof of that blind injustice which is Cary's point of departure as a novelist; and the book's events, ranging from the farcical to the horrifying, all stem from Bradgate's short views and the Carrs' overlong ones.

In such careful selection and manipulation of his material, Cary avoids wherever possible any direct statement of his intentions; a study of his manuscripts shows that again and again a directly explanatory passage, either in the author's own words or in the speech of a character, is replaced in the revision by new actions, sometimes performed by characters invented for the purpose. Musa,

Ibu and Oya, in *The African Witch*, all came into existence in this way. Cary worked repeatedly over each manuscript, determined not only that everything in it should tell, but that everything should tell by telling a story. Great concentration and economy result from this fusion of image and idea.

A study of Cary's manuscripts proves his seriousness as an artist; it is not easy to decide if it proves his success. The magazine editors who rejected his early stories did so on the grounds that they were too concentrated for pleasurable reading. 'They wanted more fluff' was Cary's own comment. His early novels were just as bony. In later years, Cary deliberately concealed the anatomy of his books beneath incidents whose relevance to the central idea is not nearly as plain as it would have been in one of his African novels. Whether the reader sees this as gain or loss depends on the expectations he brings to the reading of a novel. Because it seems (to me) as reasonable for the lines of construction to show themselves in a novel, which Cary terms a metaphysical construction, as in a building, my own preference is for the sparse and sinewy novel which can take over, in modern society, some of the functions earlier performed by poetry and the poetic drama. I prefer, that is to say, *Hard Times* to *Our Mutual Friend* and *The Longest Journey* to *A Passage to India*. But this is idiosyncratic; and while I hope I have been able to suggest that there are intrinsic merits in Cary's first few novels, I realize most readers will regard them as trial flights preparatory to the successful undertaking of the Gulley Jimson trilogy. This conclusion therefore concerns itself briefly with the formative nature of Cary's African novels.

Since Cary's experience of Africa was fixed in his memory by its isolation from the rest of his experience, it may seem surprising that his view of life should change and develop through his successive handlings of this African material. But though Cary's Africa remained a constant in his memory, Africa changed and Cary changed. Like many Liberals between the wars Cary, in a growing awareness of change in West Africa, abandoned the Edwardian principle of leaving well alone in the colonies in favour of a policy of planned aid and development. He was helped in this change of view, he tells us in the preface to the second edition of *The Case for African Freedom*, by reflection on his African experience, and much of this reflection took the form of writing novels about Africa. Since Cary's change of view in colonial matters was really part of a very rapid development in his general attitude to life, in which freedom began to appear to him as essentially dynamic and not permissive, his use of an African setting for his first few novels helped him to clarify his fundamental ideas, which were not nearly so clear as he had taken them to be at the time he began *Aissa Saved*. Accordingly, in his four African novels up to and including *Mister Johnson*, we can trace the movement, recorded also in *Power in Men* and *The Case for African Freedom*, from the negative concept of freedom as the absence of compulsion to the positive idea of it as the liberty to make a life for ourselves: 'creation in the act'.

Freedom was still freedom from compulsion for Cary when he wrote *Aissa Saved*, though the compulsion was an internal one, servitude to irrational forces. The basic injustice of life, never out of sight in the tropics where the blind beggar and the paralytic on all fours are not hustled into institutions, had to be fought, not evaded. The free man was the one who kept his wits about him and left nothing to luck or fate, and Cary had felt ever since his first weeks in Nigeria, when he had tried to encourage victims of smallpox to fight for life, that this freedom of self-reliance was the best thing Europe had to give Africa. The administrator's job was to impart the basic knowledge – sanitation, irrigation, bridge-building – which could set people free from fear and want. Missionaries of the crankier sort only sabotaged this effort when they introduced a new juju which, like the old, represented bondage to the irrational, a failure in self-reliance.

Cary felt very sure of his values when he began *Aissa Saved*. But when he finished the book, three years later, he was growing critical of the rather simple view of things with which he began. Bradgate's sensible, pragmatic approach began to seem inadequate, like sand-castles built against an incoming tide. There were, Cary admitted some years later in the Carfax preface, other solutions, 'right' for other people, to the problem of life's unfairness; and his handling of the character of Hilda Carr who in her own way helps Aissa to fight the good fight suggests that it was becoming evident to him, as he wrote, that the religious mind was not necessarily the captive mind. Without Cary himself quite understanding how it happened, Hilda's pupil, the 'possessed' Aissa, in the end stole the book from Bradgate's pupil, the self-reliant Ali. The division between the captive and the free was no longer an easy one to make.

Accordingly, Cary concerns himself in the next novel with the captivity of the seemingly free and the freedom of the seemingly captive. Thus, Marie, the American visitor from the home of the free, is an anarchist and a defender of free love, but she falls captive to a longing for security. *An American Visitor* is a political novel, and one of its themes is the captivity of anarchism compared with the freedom of good government. A manuscript note shows that this is the point of Cary's beginning the book with the crowd at the landing-stage in a state near to riot and then showing them reduced to order and tranquillity under Captain Osho of the *Black Swan*. Those like Cottee, who put themselves outside the pale, are in fact a good deal less free than characters like Gore, whom Cottee calls a tram. For Gore, while he may seem a mere cog in the administrative machine, knows that the art of administration asks daily for new decisions: for vigilant judgement and great delicacy of touch, just like the game of spillikins which one of the tin-miners derisively terms it. The service of the State is freedom to Gore, though not the perfect freedom that Bewsher makes it. A mixture of the autocrat and the anarchist, Bewsher is Cary's first attempt to resolve the tension, perhaps a personal tension, which had appeared during the writing of *Aissa Saved*, between responsibility and abandon. Even when Bewsher is killed, the reader is left with the hope of such a reconciliation being perpetuated in the marriage of Marie and Gore.

There is no such hope to be found anywhere in *The African Witch*, which is a sad book. Because its setting took Cary back to a time in his African career when he had not felt the Bewsher-like freedom he enjoyed in Borgu, and because it was built from the ruins of a book undertaken long before *Aissa Saved*, *The African Witch* scarcely contains a free character. Even Schlemm is prepared to sacrifice Dryas to his compulsion to believe in fundamental human goodness; he refuses to see the plain truth about his converts though it is literally before his eyes in the shape of a large piece of sticking plaster. The level-headed Judy surrenders herself more than once to jealousy. Elizabeth, for all her pride and power, falls into the palace trap because of her jealous infatuation with Akande Tom. Worst of all, Cary's own imagination is less free here than in any of his books: the characters are for the most part studied as psychological case-histories, the victims of their obsessions; there is none of the warmth of interest which brings Aissa or Bewsher to life.

Castle Corner, although it was not published until 1938, had taken shape in Cary's mind some years earlier, and is probably the book dealing with 'English tribes, pagans and witch-doctors', which he mentioned to Edwardes as early as January, 1934. It thus represents a natural development from the study of a pagan man in *An American Visitor*. Bewsher had taken possession of that book, as Aissa had in some degree done in its predecessor, and now Cary tried the experiment of giving his characters their head from the start. 'I meant to create characters and leave them to act; characters conceived with those springs of action which seemed to me most important in all character, working out their fates, in a world charged throughout with freedom and individuality, and the consequences of that inescapable freedom' (Carfax preface, p. 6). As a result, the book's general meaning, its significant pattern of events, is hard to make out. Reviewers missed it entirely at the time; but it is possible to discern it faintly now that we can see the book as part of Cary's entire work as a novelist. To oversimplify, *Castle Corner* is a book about the will to live; and the very act of giving his characters their head heightened Cary's awareness of the power in everyone's springs of action, an awareness which he had only temporarily lost when he went back to *Alade* for *The African Witch*, and which was to inform all his subsequent books. This vitality is seen in nearly all the characters in *Castle Corner*. Felix Corner may appear merely to vegetate, but all the time he is 'going plant' in the squalid Laka store he is leading an intense and rich mental life. A character such as Bridget, who appears at first to be a prey to an obsession, the frightening image of herself as a murderess, turns out to be guided by a much more positive force, the determination to get wealth and power for her child whose illegitimacy (his father is a young man of the Corner family, Cleeve) would otherwise leave him in poverty and obscurity.

Most of the book is concerned with Cleeve, and his cousin Harry (or Cock) Jarvis; and so with their springs of action. The cousins are morally differentiated – Cleeve's upbringing has made him thoroughly selfish, while Jarvis has a pronounced sense of duty – but they share a 'concentration of nervous life' which carries Cleeve through a series of Protean experiments with his own personality – the young blood, the aesthete, the pro-Boer liberal – and makes the empire-building Jarvis add a vast new area to the red on the map. The creative energy of both young men is contrasted with the inner vacuum of the only character in the book who is quite without – or, more accurately, who completely loses – the will to live, Phil Feenix. To gratify his half-crazed cousin, Slatter, whose own driving force is the determination to get possession of Castle Corner, Phil gives up in turn his ambitions to be a missionary and to go into the Army. He settles down to the job of Slatter's agent with no interest in life except his cousin's ghoulish ambitions, until nothing but whiskey can bring back the semblance of vitality, 'the energy and life of the fungus under a cellar which splits the pavement to reach the light and air'. In a final despair after his marriage to Slatter's half-witted daughter, he shoots himself.

In *Castle Corner* Cary thus explores the nature of personal freedom and discovers that the seemingly free may be the captives of their own purposelessness, whereas those who seem subservient to an idea or a code are often creatively free. He had already treated this theme in *An American Visitor*; and *Castle Corner*, by its historical setting, gave him the chance to work out one aspect of the matter which had troubled him in writing that book. During the thirties, the ideas of the men Cary had admired in Nigeria were becoming demoded, and their achievement belittled or even decried. Was personal freedom always at the mercy of the time spirit? A manuscript note shows that Cary tried to present Bewsher as a man whose principles could not date, because he lived in the moment: 'Bewsher enjoys life at the moment and understands that life is an art – that progress, etc., beside the point – that men and society are constructions – works of art' (P12). Yet while Bewsher is not necessarily the product of one generation's outlook (as Cottee maintains he is), he falls victim to changes which result in him, like Cock Jarvis, being 'smashed by the zeitgeist'. So, in *Castle Corner*, Cary is still turning over this problem of a possible limit to individual freedom. And his conclusion seems to be that human actions are no more the product of that 'blind thrust' of which Felix speaks than Cézanne was the product of Post-Impressionism. Jarvis's march into Daji, 'an original and simple act of imagination' is as much 'beyond headquarters' reach of ideas as Cézanne's pictures in the same year were beyond that of the Salon jury'. Cary's own reading in anthropology and reflections on his African experience were convincing him, about this time, that primitive peoples were not helpless victims of superstition and custom, a body of ideas as compelling as the European zeitgeist was held to be. In an unpublished article on 'Primitive Freedom' (N85), he maintained that the body of beliefs and customs found in tribal society was itself a creation of free minds and so subject to the attack of the new generation, which would have a fresh vision of things. The conservative were defending their own creation, truths once fresh and vital to them, and not mere custom. Accordingly, the truth as they conceived it, though it might be the next generation's error, made them free.

The writing of *Castle Corner* thus helped Cary to move away from novels structured by the contrast between the captive (whether captive to a time-spirit or a tribal god) and the free, to novels built out of the conflict of individual visions. The captive do not disappear entirely from his work – Phil Feenix is a leading character

in *Castle Corner, Charley is My Darling* is about the shades of the
prison house, and Cary's last novel is entitled *The Captive and the
Free* – but the tragic irony of *Daventry, Cock Jarvis, Tottenham,
Aissa Saved, An American Visitor* (in part) and *The African Witch,* is
replaced by the comedy of freedom: a conflict of vision with vision,
of the individual with society, of desire with hard fact, which must
continue as long as the characters have breath in their bodies, for the
reasons that they are condemned to be free.

Mister Johnson is Cary's first real comedy of freedom. Its hero is in
some degree the completion of a triad, the natural outcome of the
dialectic between self-surrender and responsibility in Cary's first
three novels. Mister Johnson has scanty education, no good habits,
and no well-conditioned reflexes. He certainly has none of the sense
of duty instilled into Ali. Yet his responses to the impulse of each
moment are not surrenders to the irrational. Other characters in the
book make such surrenders from time to time: Benjamin, Celia.
But Johnson's impulses are those of the artist, the maker. Experiences
are never pushed to the back of his mind and allowed to go bad
there, because they are transformed immediately through self-
expression in song or action. Nor is he cast down for long when
his efforts come to nothing; there are plenty more ideas where the
last came from, and, like Gulley Jimson, he is always ready to
go on to the next thing.

The extent to which Cary's concept of personal freedom developed in the late thirties can be seen in the way he handles race
relations in *The African Witch* and *Mister Johnson*. In the former book,
the contrast is mostly between normal and psychotic behaviour.
Only occasionally does Cary indicate that another contrast exists
between imaginative and unimaginative behaviour; for example,
Fisk, the A.D.O., drops his official, race-conscious manner towards
Aladai when a chance remark by the other man causes him to associ-
ate Aladai with a Negro schoolfellow. This contrast between the
imaginative and the unimaginative becomes a leading theme of
Mister Johnson. Whereas the sensible characters in the former
novel are free *from* the complexes which make race relations clumsy,

Johnson is free *to* create his own vision of Rudbeck as his collaborator on the Fada road; and in so doing he frees Rudbeck's imagination, so that he in turn comes to see Johnson creatively, as a person. The result is a story in which captivity is led captive.

The world of *Mister Johnson* is built out of Cary's memories of his last tour in Borgu. It was a time of inventive freedom framed between a period of oppressive responsibility, vividly described in the letters of his previous tour, and the difficult first years of his return to England, when he often felt he had abrogated responsibility for the sake of a freedom which had turned to bondage. During this last tour, in his dealings with Africans such as Musa and Tasuki and the Emir, whom he began to know for the first time as individuals and not just as 'these people', Cary discovered that the freedom which the Kiplingesque white man had to give Africa – the freedom of self-reliance based on knowledge – was matched and balanced by another kind of freedom that Africans had to give to the expatriate living with them: the creative freedom of those who live in the minute, improvising new songs and new dance rhythms, or making an inspired choice of the moment to thrust the big surf boat towards the breakers. Above all this African art of living consisted in an amazingly fruitful response to other people, creative of acts and gestures which were still fresh in Cary's mind twenty years later, a source of inspiration as well as a benediction.

List of Sources

UNPUBLISHED MATERIAL

In the James Osborn Collection of Joyce Cary's papers in the Bodleian Library, Oxford:

Novels set in Africa:

Daventry.
Cock Jarvis.
Alade and Mission Story.
Sequels to *Castle Corner.*
Also manuscripts of the published novels.

Plays set in Africa:

Happy Valley.
The King is Dead, Long Live the King.
Film script:
Men of Two Worlds.

Short Stories:

'Adamu.'
'Guda.'
'Marching as to War.'
'A Pagan Man.'
'The Raft.'
'Railway Camp.'
'T.R.' (N85)
'Too Good to be True.'
Also manuscripts of the published short stories.

Articles and broadcasts:

'The Approach, the Formal Construction, the Style.'

'Article on Africa.'

'Joyce Cary,' in *Signature*, a West-Country magazine of the arts, 12 June, 1955 (a broadcast in which Cary took part).

'Form and Meaning.'

(Unpublished) Preface for an American edition of *The African Witch* (N85).

'Primitive Freedom' (N85).

'Unfinished Novels.'

Also manuscripts of the published articles.

Notebooks:

A great number of these have entries relevant to Cary's 'African' novels and books about Africa. Complete short stories and articles in the notebooks have been listed above.

Letters and Personal Documents:

These include all Joyce Cary's letters to his wife; his correspondence with his American publisher; his Paris diary and his Borgu diary; a number of personal papers; and letters from colleagues in the Political Service.

Reviews:

Collected press-cuttings of reviews of Cary's books.

Official Papers in the Divisional Office, Bussa, and in the Nigerian National Archives at Kaduna and Ibadan:

The most relevant are:

Annual Reports on Bauchi Province, 1914, 1915, 1916.

Annual Reports on Borgu Division, 1918, 1919.

Annual Report on Muri Province, 1916.

Borgu Court minute-book.

Handing-over Notes, Borgu Division, 1919.

History of Gombe Emirate, by T. F. Carlyle, 1914.

Kaiama District Assessment Report, 1919.

Quarterly Report on Muri Province, September, 1916.

Yashikera District Assessment Report, 1919.

Other Information:

Supplied by Mr Michael Cary; Mr J. Chartres; Mr Cary J. Clark; Mr .H W. Cowper; Mr P. R. Diggle; the late Mr H. S. W. Edwardes, and Mrs Edwardes; Mr G. W. Izard; Mrs A. McClean; Mr S. Milburn; Dr B. Moiser; Mr O. H. Morris; Mr E. L. Mort; Mr C. Newbury; Sir Heneage Ogilvie; Mr G. Parmenter; Professor Mark Schorer; Captain F. W. Taylor; Mr C. E. T. Whitting; Professor Andrew Wright; Mr E. S. Pembleton.

PUBLISHED MATERIAL

By Joyce Cary:

Books:

The African Witch, 1951 (Carfax edition).
Aissa Saved, 1952 (Carfax edition).
An American Visitor, 1952 (Carfax edition).
Art and Reality, 1958.
Britain and West Africa, 1946; revised edition, 1947.
The Case for African Freedom, 1941; revised and enlarged edition, 1944.
Castle Corner, 1952 (Carfax edition).
Mister Johnson, 1952 (Carfax edition).
Power in Men, 1939.
Prisoner of Grace, 1952.
Spring Song, 1960.

Short Story:

'Buying a Horse.' *Punch,* 2 December 1953.

Articles:

'Africa Yesterday: One Ruler's Burden.' *The Reporter,* 15 May 1951.
'Catching up with History.' *The Nation,* 16 October 1954.
'Christmas in Africa.' *Esquire,* XL, December 1953.

'A Conversation with Joyce Cary.' *Tamarack Review*, Spring 1957.

'Joyce Cary.' An interview in *Writers at Work*, edited by Malcolm Cowley. Reprinted from *The Paris Review*, 1958.

'Joyce Cary's Last Look at His Worlds.' *Vogue* (U.S.) 15 August 1957.

'The Most Exciting Sport in the World.' *Holiday*, XXI, June 1957.

'My First Novel.' *The Listener*, 16 April 1953.

'A Novel is a Novel is a Novel.' *Adam International Review*, XVIII, 1950. Reprinted from *The New York Times Book Review*.

'A Novelist and his Public.' *The Listener*, 30 December 1954.

'The Novelist at Work' (discussion with David Cecil). *Adam International Review*, XVIII, 1950.

'On the Function of the Novelist.' *The New York Times Book Review*, 30 October 1949.

'Policy for Aid.' *Confluences*, IV, 1955.

'Speaking of Books.' *The New York Times Book Review*, 26 June 1954.

'The Way a Novel gets Written.' *Adam International Review*, XVIII, 1950. Reprinted from *Harper's*, CC, February 1950.

Preface:

Denys Craig: *Man in Ebony*, 1950.

By other writers:

(Books marked with an asterisk are books on Africa owned by Joyce Cary which he either annotated or made recognizable use of in his writings)

★ R. E. Bennett: *Nigerian Studies*, 1910.

★ C. Cyril Claridge: *Wild Bush Tribes of Tropical Africa*, 1922.

James S. Coleman: *Nigeria: Background to Nationalism*, 1958.

W. R. Crocker: *Nigeria: A Critique of Colonial Administration*, 1936.

Michael Crowder: *The Story of Nigeria*, 1962.

J. D. Falconer: *On Horseback Through Nigeria*, 1911.

J. F. J. Fitzpatrick:

'A Frontier Incident.' *Blackwood's Magazine*, CXCVI, September 1914.

'Of Mending a Wire.' *Blackwood's Magazine*, CC, August 1916.

'Mr. Johnson.' *Blackwood's Magazine*, CCI, February 1917.

'News from Gurin.' *Blackwood's Magazine*, CXCVIII, September 1915.

'A Run with the Yola Drag.' *Blackwood's Magazine*, CXCVII, April 1915.

F. B. Gall: *Gazetteer of Bauchi Province*, 1920.

E. Howard Gorges: *The Great War in West Africa*, n.d.

* Herbert C. Hall: *Barrack and Bush in Northern Nigeria*, 1923.

A. C. G. Hastings: *Nigerian Days*, 1925.

* G. D. Hazzeldine: *The White Man in Nigeria*, 1904.

H. B. Herman-Hodge: *Gazetteer of Ilorin Province*, 1929.

H. B. Herman-Hodge: (under the pseudonym of Langa-Langa) *Up Against It in Nigeria*, 1922.

F. D. Lugard: *The Dual Mandate in British Tropical Africa*, 1922

* C. K. Meek: *The Northern Tribes of Nigeria*, 1925.

* F. H. W. Migeod: *Through Nigeria to Lake Chad*, 1924.

Walter Miller: *Reflections of a Pioneer*, 1936.

* F. J. Moberley: *Military Operations: Togoland and the Cameroons*, 1931.

A. Victor Murray: *The School in the Bush*, 1929; revised edition, 1936.

Margery Perham: *Native Administration in Nigeria*, 1937.

Margery Perham: *Lugard*, Vol. I, 1956; Vol. II, 1960.

* Albert Schweitzer: *On the Edge of the Primeval Forest*, 1922.

* P. Amaury Talbot: *Life in Southern Nigeria*, 1923.

C. L. Temple: *Native Races and their Rulers*, 1918.

* A. J. N. Tremearne: *The Ban of the Bori*, n.d.

Andrew Wright: *Joyce Cary: a Preface to His Novels*, 1958

Index